My Search Through Books

Satsvarupa dasa Goswami

My Search Through Books

Satsvarupa dasa Goswami

GN Press, Inc.

Persons interested in the subject matter of this book are invited to correspond with our secretary:

GN Press, Inc.
R.D. 1, Box 837-K
Port Royal, Pa 17082

Printed in the United States of America
Limited Edition: 400 copies
June 1991

ISBN: 0-911233-86-5

If a person explains anything that is not Kṛṣṇa, he simply wastes his time laboring hard without fulfilling the aim of his life.
—Cc. Ādi, 13.29, purport.

It is a qualification of the great thinkers to pick up the best even from the worst. It is said that the intelligent man should pick up nectar from a stock of poison, should accept gold even from a filthy place . . . and should accept a good lesson even from a man or from a teacher who comes from the untouchables.
—Bhag. 1.5.11, purport

Contents

Boyhood

Junior College

Bachelor of Arts

On My Own

Preface

Śrīla Prabhupāda smashed Western culture and said it was no culture at all. Yet many millions of people live in Western culture, embrace it, and are educated in it. Those who join the Kṛṣṇa consciousness movement have also been influenced by it. Therefore, devotee-writers must face the existence of Western culture in its various forms, either to expose its bankruptcy, or in some cases, to appreciate its traces of morality and God consciousness.

But what is the value of remembering nondevotee books? Didn't Śrīla Prabhupāda tell us to forget all this? Yes, he certainly did. The attitude of a preacher is summed up in this statement by Prabhodānanda Sarasvatī Ṭhākura: "My dear Sir, I know you are a learned scholar who has read many books. I humbly bow before you placing a straw in my teeth. But although you are a great *sādhu,* I humbly request you to please kick out all this rascaldom, all this hogwash, and listen instead to the philosophy of Lord Caitanya." A similar mood is expressed by Nārada Muni in *Śrīmad-Bhāgavatam:* "Those words which do not describe the glories of the Lord, who alone can sanctify the atmosphere of the whole universe, are considered by saintly persons to be like a place of pilgrimage for crows. Since the all-perfect persons are inhabitants of the transcendental abode, they do not derive any pleasure there" (*Bhāg.* 1.5.10).

When we took to Kṛṣṇa consciousness under Prabhupāda's direction, we threw out all of our past conditioning and entered into the spiritual world. But as the Kṛṣṇa consciousness movement spreads around the world, it has to contend with Western culture. If someone asks us, "What do you think of Shakespeare's plays?" it will not do to reply, "Who is Shakespeare?" People demand an explanation and evaluation, not just a categorical rejection. After all, many sincere persons have the conviction that there is something spiritual, profound and courageous in the writers they read. We will have to show that we also know the depth of those writers, and in some cases, sympathize by admitting that we too have been influenced by them.

When I first met Śrīla Prabhupāda in 1966, I was very attached to favorite authors. I expressed this to Prabhupāda. It would have hurt too much if he completely rejected them all as useless. When I presented their cases and said that they seemed to me to be God conscious in their own way, Prabhupāda sympathetically replied that their God consciousness was in their sincerity.

Newcomers to Kṛṣṇa consciousness have roots in Western culture, and even those who have been practicing *bhakti-yoga* for a few decades are still affected by the Western tradition. One time, when Śrīla Prabhupāda was taking a walk in Boston, he stopped for a few moments in front of a toy store window. I pointed out to Prabhupāda that the toys were mostly battleships and guns. I said, "This is what we played with as children instead of Rādhā-Kṛṣṇa dolls. Does this have an effect on us now?" Prabhupāda replied that *the impressions are there.* This doesn't mean that we have to delve into the *māyā* of Western literature all over again. After receiving a treasure chest, why put it aside in search of a plastic trinket? Yet it is not wrong to come to terms with our past, especially once we are committed to Kṛṣṇa consciousness.

The purpose of my book is therefore mostly a warning that there is nothing of enduring value in Western nondevotional literature. I hope that it can serve as an explanation to those who are not yet acquainted with Kṛṣṇa consciousness but who are attached to Western literature. It may also please devotees to take a look down "memory lane" without danger, to reinforce their Kṛṣṇa conscious convictions.

There is a more personal reason for this book. I am drawn back to my own past and I want to purify it. I will tell of my search, naming the authors who helped me to cope with life. I will experience again why I had to go beyond them. I hope that this will convince others that they do not themselves have to read such authors in the search for truth.

I intend to go through the past honestly, so that the victory I will tell—of the supremacy of Kṛṣṇa consciousness—will not seem merely theoretical or dogmatic. May *My Search Through Books* please the Vaiṣṇavas. Although the subject matter is somewhat odd for a Kṛṣṇa conscious book, it is also odd and unprecendented that people born in *mleccha* civilizations can take to Kṛṣṇa consciousness. Therefore, I hope I can come through this adventure with memoirs and commentaries in the disciplic line of the Six Gosvāmīs and Śrīla Prabhupāda.

1

Boyhood

I

Coming Back?

I remember baby books. One was Davy's Day, *with simple drawings and one-liners like, "Davy rides his tricycle," and, "Davy takes his cod liver oil." There was another, more complicated book with fine drawings about a baby. It had a problematic section—the father came home and the mother was feeding the baby in his highchair, but the baby spit out his food. Everyone was displeased with him and he started to cry. It was a heavy story. There was also a book called* Chatterbox, *about a duck who talked a lot. My father called me chatterbox: "Hey, Chatterbox, don't talk so much."*

Will I have to come back in another life to go through this again? Śrīla Prabhupāda writes, "If in this life I am trying to become a devotee, this does not mean that in my many past lives I was one-hundred-percent pious . . . A devotee always prays, 'For my misdeeds, may I be born again and again; but my only prayer is that I may not forget Your service'" (*Bhāg*. 3.25.40, purport).

(2)

But that means again suffering pains in the womb of a mother, again not knowing how to control the body, not knowing what life is for, having to learn to read again. I read *Davy's Day* in America during World War II. But who knows where I will be in my next life? I may be raised as an illiterate, or born as a fox terrier in Switzerland. Or an African tsete fly.

I cannot refrain from remembering *Davy's Day*, so at least let me use it in the service of self-realization. Kṛṣṇa supplies memory, and by His grace we may be prevented from repeating an old mistake by remembering the past.

II

The Return of the Lost Servant

William Wigglesworth *was a story about a small boy who had lost his little dog. The whole book was about William asking people, "Have you seen my dog?" No one could find the dog. Finally, he met a man who had a big house filled with dogs. Was William's dog in there? You turned the page and there was a double spread of a whole house filled with dozens of dogs. It would take me a while to find it, but there, in one corner, was William Wigglesworth's little dog! I read it again and again: loving a dog, losing a dog, searching for the dog, and meeting many people.*

I want to speak as a competent instructor and counselor. I do not want to be condescending toward the old memories, but neither do I want to create a "pilgrimage for crows."

Reading *William Wigglesworth* was sweet, like "going home." You find your lost relationship with Him after many lifetimes and adventures. The soul finds shelter in a corner of Kṛṣṇa's house.

III

On the Front Stoop

There was a family down the block named the Fox's. Their mother sold and traded comic books as a way to make money. All the kids on 76th Street in Queens used to trade comics and sit on the front steps for hours reading. You would read one and then pass it to someone else and take theirs, Superman, Batman, Wonderwoman, Little Lulu, Archie . . .

Even up until the last minute on the day our family was moving away from Queens, I was still sitting reading comic books.

Someone said, "You moving today?"

"Yeah. This is our last day." We went on reading, and then I gave the Fox's some of my comic books and they gave me some of theirs.

Reading *Śrīmad-Bhāgavatam* can become easy if you are in the right mood. Today I was in the right mood. Myself and two other devotees are taking a break from our preaching and travels. We are in a secluded part of Ireland where the only sound is the wind and the surf. Sitting on the floor, I hold the book and I am thankful. I am reading in the Fourth Canto, the Kumāras speaking to Mahārāja Pṛthu.

You have to relax, preferably in good company, as we did on the front stoop in Queens. Read *Śrīmad-Bhāgavatam* the way you used to read comic books, with leisure, with friends, fully absorbed like a child or a devotee of Kṛṣṇa. Śrīla Prabhupāda says that reading is as good as active service.

IV

Reg'lar Fellas

Another book was Reg'lar Fellas in the Army. *It was a series of panel cartoons about kids playing that they were in the army. One kid wore a kitchen pot as a helmet and he carried a walkie talkie made of an empty can with a string. In between the panel cartoons, there were full-page photos of U.S. Army activities, tanks, planes, soldiers. One was a photo of an infantryman, charging with his bayonet forward. It looked like he was coming out of the picture to stab you, and the caption said that he was "in the finest tradition of the American military man." I used to reread it often,* Reg'lar Fellas. *The idea was that you shouldn't be a sissy. When you grow up, you too can be in the army. My father sent that book home, and my mother wanted me to read it.*

My mom and dad wanted me to be a regular fellow. That is why they got me that book, and that is also why my dad sent me two pairs of boxing gloves from his ship in the Pacific. I am trying to get to the bottom of this memory but I can't. Maybe later it will make more sense. Otherwise, let it go into oblivion, the boys with their kitchen pot-helmets and their play military headquarters made from orange crates, and their dog tagging behind them . . . me leafing through the over-sized, hard-bound book again and again in our apartment in Queens, gone and never to return again exactly like that. Reading *Reg'lar Fellas* was my participation in the Great Events of World War II. But as Śrīla Prabhupāda writes, warning me:

> The whole material creation is a *jugglery of names* only; . . . The buildings, furniture, cars, bungalows, mills, factories, industries, peace, war . . . [are] of no more significance than the babble of sea waves. The great kings, leaders and soldiers fight with one another in order to perpetuate their names in history. They are forgotten in due course of time, and they make a place for another era in history. . . . those who are fixed in perfect reality are not at all interested in such false things.
>
> —*Bhāg.* 2.2.3

V

Tell Me About God

I had a book called Tell Me About God. *It told how God created the trees, the land, and everything else. Another book was called* Tell Me About Jesus. *It had nice illustrations. We had a Christmas book with carols in it, and I remember sitting on the couch singing those hymns aloud to myself. I was partly enjoying my own singing, and partly knowing that they were "holy" songs. It made me feel angelic, like the holy angels in the book, to sing those carols. My mother walked by and appreciated my singing. I played it up for her too, and kept on singing, "O little town of Bethlehem, how still we see you lie . . . "*

This Christmas book had the story of the fir tree by Han Christian Andersen, with wonderful pictures. There was a little fir tree, and he was dissatisfied with his life in the forest. When he grew up, he was chopped down, decorated for the holiday, and then thrown to the fire. Before he died, he told the mice in the attic, "I should have been satisfied with my lovely life in the forest." There was also the story of a boy who had nothing to offer to Christ. "What shall I give Him? I don't have gold, I don't have a lamb. I know, I'll give Him my love." I loved that Christmas book and read it again and again, especially the illustrations.

We also had a big Catholic Bible in our house, but I never saw anyone reading it.

Śrīla Prabhupāda often commented on the importance of the first influences upon a child, especially for Kṛṣṇa consciousness.

> *Śrīla Jīva Gosvāmī remarks in this connection that every child, if given an impression of the Lord from his very childhood, certainly becomes a great devotee of the Lord like Mahārāja Parīkṣit. . . .* Mahārāja Prahlāda also advises that such impressions of a godly relation must be impregnated from the beginning of childhood, otherwise, one may miss the opportunity of the human form of life, which is very valuable, although it is temporary like others.
>
> —*Bhāg.* 1.12.30

Kṛṣṇa conscious parents deliberately bring a child into the world to give it a spiritual education. Often this appears to them to be a thankless task. After carrying their child before the temple Deities of Rādhā and Kṛṣṇa for years, and holding the infant up before the Tulasī, worshiping and chanting with them, the children often grow up to reject their upbringing, usually as teenagers. But it is likely that persons brought up in a devotional home will remember it again sooner or later, at least before death.

(10)

My own upbringing was secular. Religious obligations were fulfilled just by attending church on Sunday. My mother forced me, so there was no question of not going. If I missed even one Sunday Mass, it was a mortal sin. My mother, sister, and I would walk together to St. Clare's church through "the village," the ladies wearing their 1950s dresses and hats, and me in my dress-up clothes. After Mass, Sunday morning would be spent reading the funny papers, lounging around or playing, and in the evening, we would watch the Colgate Comedy Hour on TV.

In our house, we never spoke of an afterlife. Who would bring up such a topic? If I ever did ask a religious question as a child, it was answered in one or two sentences by my mother, usually followed by a cynical joke about the "freeloader" priests from my father.

My impression of religion, therefore, was that it was a part of family and social life. It was important in its own way, but definitely limited to a small compartment. Neither was it particularly joyful. But my superficial roots in spiritual life do not sadden me. I am simply happy that I met Śrīla Prabhupāda. My childhood misadventures with religion seem to me like humorous tales in someone else's life, like watching a TV situation-comedy. Upbringing is important, but whether you have spiritual training or not, you can still receive the mercy of the Supreme Lord *whenever* you meet His merciful representative.

In the *Nectar of Devotion,* Śrīla Prabhupāda states that according to Rūpa Gosvāmī, *bhakti* is a process continued from one's previous life. "No one can take to devotional service unless he has some previous connection with it. "But," Śrīla Prabhupāda writes, "even if there is no continuity, if only by chance a person takes interest in the pure devotee's instruction, he can be accepted and he can advance in devotional service."

That Christmas book was nice. It gave me some warm, joyful moments and a hint of spiritual peace where "the silent stars go by" in the sky of Bethlehem. It was a spiritual inkling within me, and it may have helped me in some small way to pay attention when Śrīla Prabhupāda began to sing.

VI

Newspapers

The New York Times *never entered our house, nor the "pinko"* New York Post, *nor the too-tabloidy* New York Mirror. *Of course, we read the* Staten Island Advance *every evening. But "newspaper" meant* The New York Daily News, *"New York City's picture newspaper," Republican and trashy. I grew up reading the* Daily News *editorials and slanted stories against the Commies. Each day I looked at the "Inquiring Photographer" and "Voice of the People," and other features, but the most important section was Dick Young's write-up of the Brooklyn Dodger baseball games. I appreciated his snappy style. One article began, "The twin engine airplane is a wonderful invention. Two days ago, one flew two Dodger pitchers from their farm team in Florida, and now the Brooks are off to a promising three-game winning streak." I thought Dick Young was great stuff.*

George Bernard Shaw said, "You are what you eat," and it might also be said, "You are what you read." Newspapers entangle you in the world of names. Śrīla Prabhupāda said that newspapers tell "what the rascals are doing." He considered them a waste of precious trees, especially the Sunday editions, "a big bundle of papers that everyone carries, but that are thrown in the dustbin the next morning." Giving up reading the newspaper is a sign of spiritual advancement. Śrīla Prabhupāda wrote, "Although the devotees of the Kṛṣṇa consciousness movement are quite young men, they no longer read materialistic newspapers, magazines, and so forth, for they are no longer interested in such topics" (*Bhāg.* 10.1.4, purport).

Śrīla Prabhupāda told a story about a Christian preacher in a coal mine. He could not put the fear of Hell into the miners because they were experiencing Hell every day. So the preacher said, "In Hell, there are no newspapers." "What? How horrible!"

Newspapers are a big deal. Journalists go everywhere and demand the story. Top men in government have to respond. Even as I write this comment, I am thinking, "Let me go next door and take a peek at the *Irish Times.* After all, it's the Persian Gulf War, the biggest thing that has happened in the last ten years." But if I do, I can expect to think of it over and over again, even while chanting the holy names, even in my sleep. I will think of the Gulf War instead of *Śrīmad-Bhāgavatam.* It *seems* absolutely necessary to read the current events, but it isn't.

Newspapers do not tell *why* everything is happening. They just report the movements of the flickering illusory energy *as if this were all-important.* Thus, by promoting the urgency of māyic happenings, the newspapers are in league with other perpetrators of the Big Lie. Why do people die? Why do they kill? Why do they want to accumulate more and more money? Why are the nations unjust and why are we all so selfish? Why is sin the norm? Why is there birth, death, disease and old age? Is there a solution to all suffering? There are no answers to any of these questions in the newspapers, just all the up-to-the-minute details on the current births, deaths, diseases, and old ages. The world and the newspapers are in league with ignorance. They cannot actually help anyone in the search for truth. When the first code of *Vedānta-sūtra* states, "*Athātho* . . . Now, therefore, let us inquire into the Absolute Truth"—this is an invitation to go beyond the newspapers. You will not find the Absolute Truth in the *Daily News,* or from the United Press International, or from Pravda.

In those days, I was completely molded by my parents and had no idea that I could be different from them, or that I could read a different newspaper or hold a political and cultural view separate from *The New York Daily News.* I was in *mahāmāyā,* licking my fingertips and quickly turning the pages to read Dick Young's piece on the Bums. You look back and say, "That was me? It's like a past life." But are you so advanced now? If in this life I am trying to become a devotee, that does not mean that I was always one hundred percent pious. That is not possible.

VII

Penrod

I once got a book called Colt of Destiny *as a birthday gift from my cousin Kathy. I became absorbed in it and read it all the way through. It was about a boy who had a horse. He was in a foreign country and had to cross the desert. It was a great trial and both the horse and the boy were dying of thirst. The colt was very brave and the boy too; it was their survival story.*

In school, we studied a book called Johnny Tremain. *It was a patriotic novel about the American Revolution. It was interesting even though it was a school study.*

*But one of the first books I remember reading on my own was by Booth Tarkington—*Penrod and Sam. *The heros were kids. I remember reading that book with great interest. One time, my friend Donald McLeary came over. I felt interrupted because I was absorbed in the book. We talked awhile and I mentioned that I had been reading this great book, "It's really wonderful." He said, "Book? That's stupid. What are you reading a book for?" After awhile, he said, "Let's go out." But I didn't want to go outside. "I want to look at this book some more." Donald McLeary left, saying, "You're silly." I got back into the book.*

(10)

The character, Penrod, tried to write a story. Booth Tarkington is the adult author, so he wrote the story that Penrod wrote and it is humorous for the reader. Penrod wrote these gory stories about people who fought like cops and robbers. "Sir Penfield delivered a tremendous blow to the abdomen of the enemy." Booth Tarkington was writing satirically, imagining the way Penrod would write a story. I became excited by Penrod's story and wrote one of my own, also using a satirical technique. I didn't write what was really in my heart, but about a character I called Frank Andrea, Private Eye. I did it in one of those notebooks with black and white mottled covers. On the title page I drew a police badge, "Private Eye." Frank Andrea was a private detective. He was independent of the police and a tough guy, a hero who solves crime, who doesn't cooperate with the police, but in the end who they are very grateful to for doing what they could not do. And so they join with him in a final scene of slugging where it is the cops and the private eye against the criminals. Imitating the style of Penrod, I wrote, "Frank had a license to shoot and he did."

My Penrod reminiscence is alive. Why can't my Kṛṣṇa conscious comment be as alive? I don't want to quote scripture merely in a corrective way, showing what was wrong with me in the old days. I am convinced it was wrong. I know that it is a foolish and dangerous attachment to be fond of our lives as children, but why does it appear so alive?

One answer is that it is Māyā's play. Even Lord Kṛṣṇa seemed amazed at the bewildering potency of His external energy when He was about to enter the mouth of the giant serpent, Aghāsura. Another answer is that the spirit soul is at the heart of all activities. He is moving and looking for his lost relationship with Kṛṣṇa, even when he looks in crazy places. So in Booth Tarkington and in me reading him, there are faint flickerings of spiritual life. There is light, but no fire to speak of. Yet at the sight of a light I exclaim, "How nice it was!"

In *Śrīmad-Bhāgavatam,* Vidura considers the acts of the external energy to be supreme *(Bhāg.* 3.1.16). Śrīla Prabhupāda writes, "Māyā, the supreme energy of the Lord, acted here both internally and externally." Therefore, I may lament that I was not receiving Kṛṣṇa consciousness in those books, and yet appreciate the ray of light that existed even in my *māyā*—"Know it as My illusory energy, that reflection that appears to be in darkness" *(Bhāg.* 2.9.34).

Fascination with our old *māyā* can be dangerous, like examining the beauty of a live rattlesnake. What is really there? Remember Bharata Mahārāja's compassion for his pet deer.

I must admit I have a tendency to be sentimental. I lavish affection on things that are not worthy of such love. There is also an egoistic self-love involved. "That's me! I read Penrod and I wrote my first story!" It is love for my own mortal life. But Kṛṣṇa says that "it is demoniac to be attracted by the impermanent" *(Bg.* 16.10). Śrīla Prabhupāda writes, "Accepting nonpermanent things, such demoniac people create their own gods, create their own hymns and chant accordingly."

Neither do we want to be stodgy or fail to love even someone who is insignificant and fallen, but we should love with enlightened compassion. Love by giving Kṛṣṇa to whomever you meet. Rescue that boy writing his first story. Encourage him. Tell him, "It is very nice that you like to read a book so much that sometimes you prefer to stay indoors and your playmates seem dull compared to the world of imagination and literature. Yes, there is magic there, a world of love and letters and . . . I am also happy for you that you have discovered you can write a story of your own, and when you did it, time flew by and you forgot everything else. Now understand deeply how all this comes about. It is from Kṛṣṇa, the original creator and writer of the best books. Learn from Him. Learn to write in a way that will please Him and actually help the suffering living entities who are all dying for lack of this knowledge. Penrod is only a tiny, covered-over sample of the real thing. Please consider the *Bhagavad-gītā*—it is not an ordinary book written by a poet or fiction writer. It tells us of the most wonderful place, the spiritual world, where everyone lives forever in bliss. (Kṛṣṇa sometimes comes to the earth too, and kills many demons.) 'So any person fortunate enough to hear these teachings from Kṛṣṇa or from His bona fide spiritual representative is sure to become a liberated person and get out of the darkness of ignorance' *(Bg.* 18.72, purport)."

VIII

Uncle Jim's Books

Jimmy was the youngest of my father's four brothers. I knew him quite well because when we moved to Staten Island, he was unmarried and he lived with us. I shared my bedroom with him. He used to play Italian opera and everyone else made fun of him. He liked to listen to Don Juan. In the last scene, Don Juan is in hell. The baritone singer was crying in hell, and my father and the others imitated him and made fun of Jimmy for listening to it. But he continued to listen.

When Uncle Jim moved in with me, he brought his books and put them on my shelf. One book I particularly remember was by Mark Twain. It wasn't one of his classic novels for boys. Mark Twain was an atheist and was cynical toward humankind, especially in his later years. One story in the collection was a parody on the Bible, with Mark Twain's version of Adam and Eve. It blew my mind. It was just the opposite of the Bible. Uncle Jim had other books, but I cannot remember them.

One who is raised in a nominally religious family, where belief in God is the party-line, and where love of God is not practiced spontaneously, will one day experience a crack in the foundation of official church piety. Everyone can remember his or her first whiff of atheism. The news of anti-religion does not always reach us as a negative thing. Because it smacks of rebellion, and since our experience of so-called religious life is often dull and restricted, we harken to the call that there is something else. Mark Twain also said, "Heaven for climate, hell for society." The interesting people are not teetotalers. Don Juan is in hell. So runs the easy-going version of humanistic, fun-loving atheism.

On my knees in the converted attic bedroom, I pulled out Uncle Jimmy's offbeat books from the shelf, and read what I had never dared to imagine—that the Adam and Eve story was make-believe, that there was a different point of view. How unguided I was! No one taught me about God in an interesting and formidable way; no one explained atheism. One had to stumble across these things on one's own, risk becoming confused, contaminated, and try to keep it a secret.

I would prefer a Kṛṣṇa conscious childhood. Maybe that is what I will get next time around. It will be a true head start. Instead of beginning spiritual life at age twenty-six, I could start at once chanting Hare Kṛṣṇa. I will be in good association. Religion will not be dull. Devotees will love me as spirit soul and take care of my bodily needs as well. They will help me to understand the workings of my own mind. I will learn about atheists, and I may even read Mark Twain, but not with my jaw dropping open as when I read him in this life. Yes, I prefer a Kṛṣṇa conscious childhood. And if there is an Uncle Jim who has to live with me, I will tell him, just as five-year-old Sarasvatī dāsī told the old *bābās* in Vṛndāvana, "Prabhupāda says you shouldn't smoke. Why don't you read a Kṛṣṇa conscious book instead of all these speculations and *māyā?*"

IX

Rebel Without A Cause

I remember reading Blackboard Jungle *by Evan Hunter. My friend, Charlie Joseph, became affected by it, and it made him want to become a juvenile delinquent. In the* Blackboard Jungle, *the kids called their teachers, "Hey, Teach." So after reading it, Charlie Joseph tried it out in the classroom and called a few teachers, "Hey, Teach." The James Dean movie, "Rebel Without a Cause," had that affect also. It spoke to our mentality because we also had no cause to rebel against in the 1950s. One of the big scenes in the movie was in the police station. The policeman was saying, "What's the matter with you?" James Dean started screaming, "Leave me alone! I don't know!" It was thrilling to see him scream, full of teenage defiance. When you saw a movie like that or read a book like* Blackboard Jungle, *you picked up the beat and played it out in front of your parents and teachers. Your father might be talking to you and you would be listening as his son, but part of you would be acting like James Dean or some character you had read about thinking, "My parents don't understand me. Nobody understands."*

Most of us are like sheep. We submit to anyone who "figures out" what life is all about, or who makes a cause or a slogan like, "The Rebel Without a Cause." We admire the leaders' intelligence, but we are not intelligent enough to see that actually, the heroes have not truly figured it out.

Here is what *Śrīmad-Bhāgavatam* says about misleaders:

> Persons who are strongly entrapped by the consciousness of enjoying material life, and who have therefore accepted as their leader or guru a similar blind man, attached to external sense objects, cannot understand that the goal of life is to return home, back to Godhead, and engage in the service of Lord Viṣṇu. As blind men guided by another blind man miss the right path and fall into a ditch, materially attached men led by another materially attached man are bound by the ropes of fruitive labor, which are made of very strong cords, and they continue again and again in material life, suffering the threefold miseries.
>
> —*Bhāg.* 7.5.31

It is too easy and preachy to tell everyone, "Just follow your local Hare Kṛṣṇa devotees. They are the real leaders. As for authors, kick them all out and read only Śrīla Vyāsadeva and Śrīla Prabhupāda." We want to say that, but we have to do it ourselves first. First *you* become a worthy follower. *You* read Śrīla Prabhupāda's books before you tell others to. *You* kick out *Time* magazine and TV news and movies and videos and *prajalpā.* I mean *me.* We are supposed to be the Kṛṣṇa conscious writers and readers. Let's do it. No more Evan Hunters for me.

Advice to parents from an old ISKCON student whose youth was misspent: Give your children a chance to chant and hear with you. They will thank you later. They will remember it in the end—Rāmacandra, the Pāṇḍavas, Lord Kṛṣṇa, the Supreme Personality of Godhead, the Hare Kṛṣṇa mantra, friends, reading and explaining *Śrīmad-Bhāgavatam*. But do not force it on them! Do not turn them off with boring, rambling lectures. Do not speak of sweet transcendence and then act cruelly. They will see your uncontrolled senses. Or they will see your peace in Deity worship. They will take seriously whatever you do. Let us not unnecessarily turn the children of Vaiṣṇavas into rebels without a cause.

2

Junior College

I

From Karma to Jñana

In our freshman English course, we first studied grammar and nothing else. After a few weeks of this drilling, I went up to Dr. Alexander and said, "Are we going to eventually start reading literature and writing some essays?" She said, "Oh, yes, don't worry." And then she was into the Romantic poets, reading them from an Oxford anthology. When Dr. Alexander was talking about John Keats or Shelley, she would get so excited she could barely contain herself. Her eyes would shine and she would say, "These poems are beautiful! And their view of life!" Unless you were a stone, you could not resist her conviction that the Romantic poets were rare souls who could feel such intensity and write with such depth. As much as she appreciated Shelley's love of nature and flights of language, she also loved his vision of world socialism and his attacks against the establishment. She liked all the Romantic poets and taught them with great affection and devotion. She said that Wordsworth later soured on the French Revolution and thus his poems deteriorated. But Shelley, she said, kept up his vision until the end. He and John Keats died young. Keats was not a political revolutionary, but his was the cult of beauty. He wrote, "Beauty is truth and truth is beauty. That is all you know and all you need to know."

Dr. Alexander's tastes in poetry coincided with the standard taste for what is considered great literature, so she taught it according to the syllabus, but with personal, dynamic energy. Just as a religious evangelist is moved by the spirit and wants others to accept Jesus, Dr.Alexander felt the same way about intellectualism and poetry. The poets and Dr. Alexander were moved by the spirit—and once they started talking about their love, you couldn't help but be moved too.

In an intellectual sense, the college teachers who first awakened me to knowledge were like *ācāryas;* at least they believed and loved what they taught. They had enthusiasm and potency. They came to me at a time when my mind was awakening, when I was impressionable. Previously, I had given full allegiance to my father and mother. But the feeling that Mom and Dad were the best and two wisest people in the world gradually waned, and was even broken by my father's manipulations of my life. My natural submission was now transferred into love for intellectuals and the intellectual life. It was like a conversion from what I knew of "materialistic" life to the life of spirit.

The teacher-student relationships that I entered had many admirable qualities and followed the traditional model between a teacher and a student. If I try now to criticize my first professors as "useless *jñanīs,"* my criticism becomes mixed with an affectionate bond. For example, I may also call my father a *mūḍhā* and a foolish *karmī*. Although this may be objectively correct, I must also consider that he is my father and I owe him some gratitude.

Even Śrīla Prabhupāda praised his college professors, although they were all Christian men and never taught him Kṛṣṇa consciousness. Prabhupāda attended Scottish Churches College in Calcutta where there were daily Bible classes and instructions in European civilization. Whenever Śrīla Prabhupāda remembered his professors, which he frequently did even in his last days, there was almost always a fondness.

> We respected our professors as our fathers. The relationship between the students and the professors was very good. The vice-chancellor, Professor W.S. Urquhart was a perfect and kind-hearted gentleman, with whom we sometimes joked.

Prabhupāda would recall each professor by name and subject. He told us who taught him English, Sanskrit, Philosophy, Psychology, and Economics. For example, he remembered the teaching methods of his English professor, J.C. Scrimgeour:

> While teaching English literature, he would give parallel passages from Bankim Chandra Chatterji. "Yes, yes," he would say, "your Bankim Bābū says like this." He had studied Bankim's literatures, and he compared Bankim Chandra Chatterji to Walter Scott. In those days, Dickens and Sir Walter Scott were two very great English

literary men. So he taught us those novelists, and the relationship was very nice.
—*Śrīla Prabhupāda-līlāmṛta,* Volume 1, p. 22

Prabhupāda would sometimes even quote these professors' statements as evidence in his own preaching. Urquhart's statement about a woman's brain, his Economics professor's lecture on Marshall's Theory (that family affection is the impetus for economic development) and other passages and teachings, are well-known to Prabhupāda's disciples. They all came from the faculty at Scottish Churches College.

Should I now completely break that bond with my first professors and negate any feelings? No, those *jñanīs* were my first teachers and it was not all evil. The pure enthusiasm and the love of knowledge that they conveyed is something worth keeping. Cāṇakya Paṇḍita teaches that we should accept good instruction, even if it comes from low-class persons. And *Śrīmad-Bhāgavatam* informs us that we may accept as gurus some of the animals and birds because of the valuable lessons they give us. If a dog can be a guru, why not a lover of English poetry and a lover of ancient history?

As for the poets themselves, the "great souls," I cannot help but speak from my present state of consciousness. I find them sorely lacking. I remember a devotee asking Prabhupāda after a public lecture, "What about Rabindranath Tagore, is he a great poet?" Prabhupāda said that he was great for the materialists, "but we are interested in the poets Vyāsadeva and Vālmikī." We are interested in the

Six Gosvāmīs and the other Vaiṣṇava poets, and in any poet who continues that tradition, "in pursuance of the Vedic version." With the Romantic poets, we recall Prabhupāda's statement that their sincerity is their God consciousness. Their mysticism is mostly pantheistic, to put it in philosophical terms. They see God in nature, in people's hearts, in goodness, in a world vision of peace and happiness. But God the person is rarely, if at all, touched upon. Hayagrīva dāsa was hardpressed in his *BTG* essays, to actually find Kṛṣṇa consciousness in William Blake, Wordsworth, and so on. Whatever lines he found about God having a personal form, were ambiguous and could be taken in different ways. They were definitely not talking about Kṛṣṇa in Vṛndāvana.

As long as I am in this body, no doubt I will remember at least fragments of their gorgeous music—like Shelley's poem to the skylark, beginning, "Hail to thee blithe spirit! Bird thou never wert!" And lines from Keats, "Sometimes I have been half in love with death . . . " and Byron's, "She walks in beauty as the night." And Wordsworth's, "My heart leaps up when I behold a rainbow in the sky." These lines go through the blood like cadences of spirit, music. Theirs is the beauty of language, the pursuit of truth and justice. More overt religious expressions are found in William Wordsworth's "Intimations of Immortality," as when he described babies being born "trailing clouds of glory from God who is their creator."

I don't want to speak more about it here for fear of sounding condescending toward these poets. Certainly they endured great austerities and achieved great heights. We also have to consider that they appeared at a certain time and place, and despite all their conditioning and the conventions in which they lived, they achieved what they did and turned toward freedom in spirit. They were doing what Prabhupāda says every soul wants to do, get beyond the confines of the body and the universe to attain the light and the spirit. Poetry that is purifying and leads to sublimity is good, but the last instruction of the *Bhagavad-gītā* is the last word in all morality and religion: "Surrender unto Kṛṣṇa." This is what I now need to hear in poetry, and I dare say this is what we all need. Those words which do not describe the name, fame, and form of Śrī Kṛṣṇa, the Supreme Personality of Godhead, are like decorations of a dead body. On the other hand, poems sincerely glorifying Kṛṣṇa and the devotees according to *paramparā,* even if not written or composed in elegant language, are appreciated by those who are thoroughly honest. Poets of the world, whoever you may be, please nourish us from the Source!

II

World Literature

Dr. Alexander told us that theologians cannot answer the question, "Why is there evil in the world if God is good?" She said this in the same way she would say that Shelley is a great poet or that you should write your essays with proper grammar. I thought that her statement was true and that there was no God conscious explanation for evil in the world. It made me think that if you went to a theologian and said, "Why is there evil in the world if God is good?" he would say, "I don't know."

She also used to satirize priests when they occurred in literature. When we studied Canterbury Tales *by Chaucer, she took advantage of the human portraits of the priests and made them laughable hypocrites and buffoons.*

In her world literature class, we also studied Voltaire, a real Church-basher. His motto was, "écrasez l'infamie," *which means "rub out the infamy." For Voltaire, one of the infamies was the Church. In his play* Candide, *he made fun of the philosopher Leibneitz, who said that whatever happens in this world, it is still the best of all possible worlds because God made the world. But Voltaire attacked this. He wrote* Candide *just after an earthquake killed many thousands of people in Lisbon. In*

Candide, *many horrible things happen to the hero, yet he remains a foolish optimist based on the philosophy which he learned from his professor, Doctor Pangloss (a slightly disguised version of Leibneitz). Doctor Alexander relished attacking this optimistic philosophy, "the best of all possible worlds."*

We also read a book by the French novelist Émile Zola, called Germinal. *He wrote about the capitalist oppression of the mining industry. It was a heavy social message, written from the grassroots viewpoint. In Zola's novel, the Church was definitely not a spiritual force, but was included among the oppressors who squelched out the attempts for happiness by ordinary people in the world.*

Then we read a short novel by Thomas Mann, Death in Venice, *which was filled with the symbolism of death. Reading it was like a game, and you were supposed to see the different ways that death appeared in the story, such as when a man passed by on the street, or when a young boy was admired but then his teeth showed that he would not live long. Everything was about death.*

Recalling the Great Books on Dr. Alexander's syllabus, I am surprised how many of them had an anti-religious slant. Dr. Alexander used to say that art should not be didactic. "Didactic" was almost a dirty word in her class. If a novel overtly taught a moral or religious message, she considered it a major flaw. And yet, what was Voltaire, Zola, or even

Thomas Mann doing but teaching with a message? *Certain messages* were acceptable to Dr. Alexander; others were didactic. Thus, I encountered the big-time cynics Voltaire and Zola, who deny the truth of religious institutions. This was cynicism with teeth. Dr. Alexander helped us to appreciate the blasts at religion as truth-seeking. Within this ocean of relativity—which Śrīla Rūpa Gosvāmī describes as an ocean filled with crocodiles and sharks—I rode on the boat provided by Dr. Alexander, appreciating those authors she selected, and trusting that she was presenting the authorized, academic *paramparā*.

I cannot remember any of the students giving Dr. Alexander (or my history professor, Dr. Pessen) a formidable challenge. They mostly regarded our questions and remarks as dumb because we were only community college students living in backward Staten Island. And we were dumb. There was a right answer to every question, and only the professor knew what it was. The authors of the books we read had something specific in mind, and the teachers knew the authors' minds. If a community college student dared to disagree with an author's view of life, someone like Dr. Alexander would simply laugh. I cannot even remember anything like that happening, a student protesting about Voltaire's world view. And although we studied sections of the Bible as literature, no one ever said, "Look, I'm a Christian and we don't read the Bible as mere literature." Although the students were sometimes unruly, they were intellectually docile;

no one was a match for Dr. Alexander or Dr. Pessen. After all, whatever they said, we had to write on our exam papers in order to get a passing grade. Knowledge had a specific form and shape and we were there to gather it. Even Śrīla Prabhupāda recalls that when he was in college, he did not answer back when one of his professors criticized the Vedic theory of transmigration as insubstantial. The teacher said that since there was no witness for a person's activities at the end of life, how could karma be transferred to a next life? In recalling this, Prabhupāda said, "We were not expert at the time," so he did not protest. But since then, Śrīla Prabhupāda has taught the whole world that the witness of our deeds is the Supersoul who awards us a next life according to our karmic desires.

As Śrīla Prabhupāda's student, I have also been busy refuting my college instructor's claim that no theologians can answer the problem of why there is evil in the world. There is evil because the living entities misuse their tiny free will. God is not to blame for our misdeeds. Since we are eternal fragments of the Supreme Being, we possess a minute amount of free will, the same as Kṛṣṇa. Kṛṣṇa's infinite will is always free of any imperfection, but ours comes under the cover of material illusion. When we think, "I am as good as Kṛṣṇa, why should only He be worshiped?" then Kṛṣṇa allows us to come to the material world to carry out our dream of independence and supremacy. All that we do in material consciousness is a type of evil against the laws of God, and thus we create so much trouble and suffering for other living entities and ourselves as we transmigrate life after life. As the kind father, Kṛṣṇa comes to this world or sends His representatives, and continually gives us the compassionate message that we should give up evil and suffering and return to our original, blissful state in the spiritual world. God is not to blame for evil, nor is it a riddle why evil exists in the world of passion and ignorance.

Previously I mentioned that my college professors might be considered as gurus, but no, I cannot call them gurus. The guru is one who knows the science of God, who is himself immersed in Brahman, and who imparts this knowledge to his disciples. My history professor, Dr. Pessen, said we can "study history without looking over our shoulders." He meant that we don't have to think of a pragmatic application in order to justify the study of history. But *jñana,* or love of knowledge itself, is limited without connection to the supreme source of knowledge. If we critically scrutinize the foundations of what my professors taught, we find Darwin's evolutionary theory, the perfectability of man, and secular humanism. As a college freshman, I thought that this was the ultimate knowledge and I could not inquire further. I was satisfied. What remained for me to do, I thought, was to read and learn as much as possible, develop devotion for the traditional authors, study and master languages, philosophies, historical systems and so on. I had no concept that after exhaustive studies of knowledge, I should come to an ultimate conclusion.

III

The Artist's Vision

We read "The Open Boat," by Stephen Crane. It was about survivors from a wreck being stranded in the water. Aside from Crane's expert, realistic depiction, Dr. Alexander said that he was teaching that nature is cruel and that there is no meaning to the universe. We are all tiny living entities in this heartless universe, just as they were feeling in the boat in the middle of the vast ocean.

In our French class, we read "A Simple Heart," by Flaubert. This is a story about a simple and kind maidservant. In one episode, she is taking care of a child and they are in the field. A bull charges them and this simple-hearted lady first saves the child's life and then at the last minute, she jumps over the fence, just before the charging bull can gore her. The maidservant has a pet parrot who is very dear to her. She is also religious. So at the time of death, the "simple heart" has a vision that she is being transported to heaven, and there she beholds her parrot, as if it is the presiding deity. Flaubert was praised for his consummate artistic skill, and the story was interesting as an accurate description of a peasant woman's mind. But we also appreciated his comment—he saw religion as merely a fancy that only a simple person could believe. And even such a simple, faithful person would not see God at death, but something they thought of in this life—a parrot.

In our second year of French, we read the novel, “L’Étranger (The Stranger*), by Albert Camus. It begins,* “Aujourd’hui la mère est mort *(Today mother died, or was it yesterday? I really can’t be sure).” This was a classic existential novel in which the character is estranged from life, and a stranger to himself. He doesn’t know what he is supposed to do or what life is about. He cannot relate to anyone or anything. One day he is walking along the beach in the brilliant sunshine and things happen that bewilder him, and before he knows it, with little pretext, he kills someone. There isn’t really any reason for him to do it. So he is arrested and given the death sentence. At the very end, a priest is sent to give him last rites, but the stranger says, “Go away, I have no use for you.” That is how Camus felt about religion.*

At the time I read these books, I was in love with literature. I thought it was a great way to go through college. Other studies seemed dry by comparison. Literature was talking about life and people, and it was created in artistic ways by artists, novelists, and poets. I wanted to be part of it and dedicate my life to it.

When I was breathing the atmosphere of Beauty and Truth while reading the Great Authors, I was actually lost. The authors themselves were lost, as their biographies reveal. I do not want to put them down. There is some sacredness to a life, whatever you are doing. On the other hand, I just can’t let it go and say, "I loved the authors at that time. So leave it at that." If my recalling is to be a purificatory process, then I want to relive my love but correct it. Where my love was sentimental and wrongheaded, I want to speak it rightly. It is not my task to attempt to debunk all the nonspiritual writers of the world, nor to trace out impersonalism in the religious writers. I am just giving my impressions, digging at my roots. And when I see something wrong in terms of my own growth, I am correcting it here for the record. I am not equipped to knock over all the great authors to everyone's satisfaction. But I am correcting it for myself, noting it and sharing with the hope that this will be interesting and helpful to those who seek the truth.

Stephen Crane's statement that we are lost in the universe is true for him and for some others. That is all they see or know. I cannot say that Crane is lying. He is writing honestly what he knows and what he has accepted from experience. But Śrīla Prabhupāda says that such, "I think" remarks should be made privately, in the closet. It is one thing to say, "This is all I got out of life," but to create an artistic symbolism of an "open boat" and present it as the meaning for total existence—everyone stranded with no Rescuer, no meaning, no eternity—that is not fair to others. Neither is it strictly true.

So it is with Flaubert's picture of the next life as merely a foolish woman's projection of moral hopes. Granted, Flaubert was reacting against the inadequate afterlife philosophy presented by the

Catholic church, but he should have gone further. It is said in the *Śrīmad-Bhāgavatam* that no one should become a guru or parent or government leader, etc., unless he can free his dependents from death. We may also say that no one should become a poet or novelist or short story writer, etc., unless he can liberate his *readers* from death. Art is not enough. Being true to one's experience is praiseworthy, but it is not enough. No one, no matter how honest, can go beyond the four human defects without taking shelter in the Supreme.

One time, some of us told Śrīla Prabhupāda that Camus and Sartre saw life as absurd. Śrīla Prabhupāda replied, "It is absurd for him." There is a stranger, but there is also a recovered servant of the Lord. We can understand that a stranger might not want a bumbling, hypocritical priest to perform rites at the end of life. "Leave me alone." But this should not be used to deny the soul's immortality.

Artists may claim that they are not actually preaching atheism or anti-religion. That is not their responsibility. And yet, an artist must be responsible, because he is often the most influential person in a culture. When scientists invent the atom bomb, they also say that they are not responsible for how it is used. Why invent it then? For everything we do, we get a karmic reaction, either by our direct work or by our implication in sinful life. If artists are human beings like everyone else, they also need to be educated so that their art may be pure, true, and enduring.

(42)

I still love world literature. By comparison, other studies seem dry. Even philosophy improves with art. I think of a poem like Rūpa Gosvāmī's "Śrī Haṁsaduta." It is a direct perception of Kṛṣṇa's eternal pastimes, something only a pure devotee can have access to. At the same time, he has presented it with imagination, beautiful Sanskrit poetics, and charming human gestures. As that was true in the 17th Century, so writers and readers today can also depict Kṛṣṇa consciousness in literary forms. We are not going to mount a book-burning campaign against the forces of secularism. Let us create a new world literature based on the vision of the liberated sages. Why should the territory be left to the morose ones?

IV

The Village Atheist

When I began Staten Island Community College, I was still attending Sunday Mass; I was a Catholic. But two years later, when I graduated from community college, I no longer attended Mass and did not consider myself a Catholic. I never received training in theology or theism, so I was a push-over for the atheistic argument. All it took was a few atheistic jokes. The professors whom I admired so much, and who represented the intellectual world to me, chuckled at religion, and so did many of the authors that we read. They made me think that being a Catholic or religionist was on a par with reading the New York Daily News.

At this time, I also read Bertrand Russell's, "Why I Am Not a Christian." His arguments were strong, I thought, and he was an attractive figure, an old man, with indomitable spirit, "the greatest living British philosopher."

Around this time, I also started subscribing to a journal, The Free Thinker. *It was American-based, telling the history of American atheism. It used to arrive in the mail, although my mother intercepted it a few times. One day while I was nosing around in my father's bureau, I saw a couple of* Free Thinkers *in there. I men-*

tioned it to my mother, but we did not dare have any real discussion about these matters. She said, "You shouldn't read these." I said, "Well, you shouldn't intercept my mail."

One of the favorite writers in the Free Thinker *was Thomas Paine. He was a respected patriot—"Common Sense" is his famous pamphlet. He had the talent of a rhetorician and propagandist, and could write an essay to work people's emotions up, as he did in "Common Sense." He was also an atheist, and in the same spirit, he wrote anti-religious propaganda.*

The Free Thinker *held the conception that atheism means free thinking. Who wouldn't want to be a free thinker? Who wants to be an un-free thinker? Dare to be an atheist! I still had a little religion in me, a little fear that if I abandoned God, I might be sorry at the time of death. But I dared to give up my faith. Partly I did it to defy my father, to show him that I could read what I wanted.*

I was mostly a closet atheist, but on a few occasions, I came out and showed my stuff. I wrote Voltaire's motto, "Écrasez l'infamie" *on a flat rock and kept it in a prominent place in my room. I could not openly defy my mother's order to go to Sunday Mass, so I left the house to go to Mass, but then spent my time sitting in the train station. One night, after getting drunk in some of the local bars, I wrote the words, "God is dead," on a piece of paper, and slipped it under the door of St. Clare's church for the priest to see in the morning. Then I steathily backed away and trotted home.*

My atheism was not very rigorous, and sometimes I revised it. After reading Allen Ginsberg's Howl, *in which he gave long lists of everything holy—the typewriter is holy, the cockroach is holy, holy, holy, holy—I decided that I was actually a pantheist. A drunken pantheist.*

My religious life was of the lowest order, and therefore it was easily toppled. But my atheism was also not unassailable, and when I met Śrīla Prabhupāda, he easily crushed it. As he wrote in the Preface to *Śrīmad-Bhāgavatam,* "It is powerful reading matter in the Sanskrit language, and it is now rendered into English elaborately so that simply by a careful reading, one will know God perfectly well, so much so that the reader will be sufficiently educated to defend himself from the onslaught of atheists. Over and above this, the reader will be able to convert others to accepting God as a concrete principle."

I am no longer an atheist. I have a long way to go to realize God, but I am in His Kṛṣṇa consciousness movement. I beg to remain in it, and I don't want to fall. I am begging to stay to prove my love and serve with the devotees.

I know the pros and cons of the atheists' debate, but they don't seem particularly threatening or even relevant. Even the classic "proofs" of God's existence according to Western philosophy, seem to be separate from the real point. I know that I live in Kṛṣṇa's energies, and I seek each day to speak to Him and hear from Him; I chant His names; I mold my life according to the instructions of His pure devotee.

Socially and psychologically I am bound up in the Kṛṣṇa consciousness movement despite all its external faults. I seek to improve my own faults, and to be accepted by my brothers and sisters. I try to help others and in this way, on a daily basis, I experience Bhagavān Śrī Kṛṣṇa.

I have witnessed my spiritual master smashing the atheists. "You are not the master," he told a newspaper reporter. "Can you say you are master? You are a servant of Kṛṣṇa. Can you refute this?" He could not refute it, and neither can I. Nor do I want to refute it. I want to accept Kṛṣṇa's mercy.

Obviously, it is of interest to me to go through all this again and to note at least briefly, how I became an atheist and what it was. It helps me to take up my present responsibilities with more awareness. It solidifies me and I can think, "I have been through that, and I am not going back to it. It can't reach me."

We may become atheists for all kinds of funny reasons, such as to defy our parents. But it is no joke. Atheism is dangerous to the soul. It is the worst possible position to be in. It is the atheistic mentality that is killing this planet. It is the cause of war and the exploitation of earth's resources. Śrī Kṛṣṇa describes them, "They say that this world is unreal, with no foundation, no God in control." And Prabhupāda comments, "The demoniac are engaged in activities that will lead the world to destruction. . . . Such people are considered the enemies of the world because ultimately, they will invent or create something which will bring destruction to all. . . . Due to Godlessness, such weapons are invented in human society" *(Bg.* 16.9, purport).

Webster's Dictionary defines "free thinker" as, "A person who forms opinions about religion independently of tradition, authority, or established belief." Of course, the atheist is not actually free. He is not free of the modes of nature, but forced to act by combinations of goodness, passion and ignorance. Śrīla Prabhupāda notes, "The materialistic person has no knowledge that ultimately he is under the control of Kṛṣṇa. The person in false ego takes all credit for doing everything independently, and that is a symptom of his nescience" *(Bg.* 3.27, purport).

Neither is a "free thinker" immune from the four human defects: the tendency to make mistakes, the cheating propensity, illusion, and limited senses. Like all conditioned souls, the "free thinker" is like a soccer ball kicked by the modes of nature up and down a field without cessation. I should have noted it myself, that even when I became a free thinker, I was being pressured and molded and acted upon in many different ways. I wanted freedom, but it could not be achieved just by rubber-stamping myself "free."

Now I have it: Mādhva-Gauḍīya-Vaiṣṇava theology. It is a formidable world-class theism, anticipating all forms of atheism and agnosticism, especially the subtle, indirect doctrine known as "*advaita-vedānta.*" The Vaiṣṇava *ācāryas* also coach us how to approach direct perception of Śrī Kṛṣṇa, the Supreme Truth. So we have knowledge and devotion, *bhakti-vedānta.* And this comes down in an unbroken chain of liberated Vaiṣṇava *ācāryas.* They teach that the ultimate truth is pure *bhakti,* free of all material taints. Religious doubts still occur to me sometimes, and perhaps some of them are reactions to things I heard in my college classes, or they are my karma for some of the atheistic pranks I performed. But I know that I can weather the doubts by humbly participating in the nine-fold practices of *bhakti-yoga.* The spirit soul is always welcomed and revived there; the Supreme Lord and His devotees are always ready to take us back.

When will these unholy voices and blasphemous memories leave us? Perhaps some day. In the meantime, those of us who have survived an earlier life in which we were rascals against the Supreme, can take solace even in the fact that we acted wrongly. We are scarred but no longer naive. We are not going to follow Bertrand Russell's logic, just because he looks like a wise old gentleman smoking his pipe. The *Free Thinker* seems childish and puffed-up.

Because of what we have gone through, we have gained a toughened wisdom. We have had to pay, and we still have to pay for the blasphemies we spoke or heard, but even this deepens our attachment to seeking shelter among the Lord's devotees. When we chant and our minds go off, we slap our heads for past wrongs. As Śrīla Prabhupāda writes, "Not only should one give up past bad habits, but he must always regret his past sinful acts. This is the standard of a pure devotee" *(Bhāg.* 6.2.27, purport).

It is better to be a *nitya-siddha* who never fell to the material world. And it is better to have been born in a family of pure devotees and to never have forgotten Kṛṣṇa. But if you have come to Kṛṣṇa through "the school of hard knocks," you can at least count your blessings and roar back at the atheism in yourself and others. Kṛṣṇa has a special use for ex-atheists.

V

The Catcher in the Rye

I had a paperback edition that seems to no longer be in print. Nowadays, all of J.D. Salinger's books have classic covers on them, with simply the title, but mine had an illustration of Holden Caulfield walking away. He had a long coat on and his hunting cap on backwards. I didn't like the picture because it was too explicit; it didn't leave room for your imagination. My sister gave me the book because she thought I would like it. It was a friendly, sisterly sharing of something, not because she loved it particularly, but because she thought, "Stevie is going to like this."

It was written in natural speech with no pretensions, expressing the mind of a young man my age. Until I read Catcher in the Rye, *I wasn't used to seeing a story written like that.* Huckleberry Finn *is also straight speaking by a boy, but you don't know anyone who talks like that, backward 19th Century southern talk. But Holden was speaking like a friend you are just meeting. That is the whole appeal—there is nothing in between you and Holden, no barriers, no literary conventions. All of a sudden, you open a book and you have a friend. I used to write in my diary, "What would Holden Caulfield do in a situation like this?" Or when I was in a jam I would think, "What would Holden do?" I also started writing like that, imitating his story.*

Sometimes it takes time for a book to warm up. In Look Homeward, Angel, *Thomas Wolfe starts out describing his character's forefathers, giving detailed information about past generations. One thinks, "It is probably important, so I can't skip it. I'll just have to hang in." But Holden starts right out. He says, "I'm not going to tell you about my parents and all that David Copperfield kind of crap." It is a quick connection that stays throughout.*

When I read it around 1958, the book was already very popular. Later, I read an article by Norman Mailer in which he was reviewing contemporary writers. He wrote, "Of course, everyone loves Salinger," and then he went on to put him down. That was Mailer: "Everyone loves him, so now look at me, I am going to put him down." When there is a trend and someone is being raved about, after awhile, people start looking at him soberly and thinking, "We were infatuated with him, but he wasn't that great." I still pick up novels with blurbs on the back cover referring to Holden Caulfield. One said, "The character is a southern Holden Caulfield, only tougher, and just as funny!"

I recommended it and passed it on to my pal, John Young. He liked it and Tommy Oakland liked it too. I was enthusiastic about Catcher in the Rye, *but my English professor was not. She thought that any literature, even something you or I write, has to be judged in terms of the greatest things that have ever been written. She thought Salinger was okay, but if you were going to be a student of literature, better to be excited by some of the great works. My love for Salinger exposed my taste as being mediocre, but I liked him enough to come out of the closet and praise him, even if the company I was in might not think of him as great. I liked it regardless of social taste, and when I finished reading it, I began rereading it. It had a lot of heart, and I liked the values.*

In case someone doesn't know the story, it is written in the first person by a seventeen-year-old boy named Holden. It opens after he has just been kicked out of Pencey Prep for poor grades. It is the third prep school that he has been kicked out of. He is supposed to wait a week until Christmas vacation and then go home to his parents in Manhattan, but he decides to leave early and spend a weekend on his own in a hotel in New York City. The "plot" is what happens to him over that weekend. But that doesn't tell you *anything*. The real story is his thoughts, his sensibility, his speech—who he is. And he rambles it out on every page. One scholar stated that Holden was Christ-like, and someone else says he was like Huckleberry Finn, but that is not the point either.

Holden hates phonies and he sees them everywhere. When he sees a "F____ you" sign on a wall, he stops to rub it out and thinks how he would like to rub out the "F____ you" signs all over the world. But then he decides that it would be impossible; there are too many of them.

One scene I liked was when he met two nuns at a sandwich shop near Grand Central Station. He talks with them and gives them a big donation. Then he winds up blowing cigarette smoke in their faces and he "apologizes like a madman."

I also liked the description of his going to see the movie *Hamlet*, starring Sir Lawrence Olivier, with his brother, and sister, Phoebe:

> But I didn't enjoy it much. I just don't see what's so marvelous about Sir Lawrence Olivier, that's all. He has a terrific voice, and he's a helluva handsome guy, and he's very nice to watch when he's walking or duelling or something, but he wasn't at all the way D.B. said Hamlet was. He was too much like a goddamn general, instead of a sad, screwed-up type guy. The best part in the whole picture was when old Ophelia's brother—the one that gets in the duel with Hamlet at the very end—was going away and his father was giving him a lot of advice. While the father kept giving him a lot of advice, old Ophelia was sort of horsing around with her brother, taking his dagger out of his holster and teasing him, and all the while he was trying to look interested in the bull his father was shooting. That was nice. I got a big bang out of that. But you don't see that kind of stuff much. The only thing Phoebe liked was when Hamlet patted his dog on the head. She thought that was funny and nice, and it was.

I also liked it when Holden asked the cab driver, as they drove through Central Park where the ducks go in the wintertime? It is too long to quote, but I will give you just a little bit of it:

> "The ducks. Do you know, by any chance? I mean, does somebody come around in a truck or something and take them away, or do they fly away by themselves—go south or something?" The driver turned all the way around and looked at me. He was a very impatient-type guy. He wasn't a bad guy, though. "How the hell should I know? How the hell should I know a stupid thing like that?"
>
> "Well, don't get sore about it," I said. He was sore about it or something.
>
> "Who's sore? Nobody's sore."

Holden likes his younger sister, Phoebe. And he wants to be a "catcher in the rye."

What has this to do with Kṛṣṇa consciousness? I would say that every devotee ought to aspire to be as honest and loving as Holden. We could use more Holdens in the world. I haven't renounced my affection for *Catcher in the Rye*. I think it is a wonderful book and J.D. Salinger must have received Kṛṣṇa's mercy to write it. He must have been very sincere in his desires.

Once when I was giving a lecture at an ISKCON *bhakti-yoga* club at the University of Maryland, I mentioned Holden Caulfield. I forget exactly what my point was, but it was like making a reference to a friend and assuming that the audience liked him. But after the lecture, a girl raised her hand and said, "Don't forget, Holden Caulfield was the son of rich parents and didn't have to worry about his economic situation." She went on to make a Marxist argument. I thought, "Now do I have to get into a big argument defending Holden Caulfield?" I said, "When the book was written, Holden was only seventeen years old, so he was too young to have to deal with that." I thought of something else to tell her, although I didn't dare say it—"Maybe Holden Caulfield could have become a devotee of Kṛṣṇa."

VI

On The Road

The first impression I recall of Jack Kerouac was seeing the photo of him in the New York Times, *looking beat. Kerouac didn't use the word beatnik himself, but beat. Beat expressed the attitude of a generation that was tired of war, tired of hassle. I saw Kerouac speaking at Hunter College, "Is the* New York Times *beat?" John Young, Tommy Oakland, and I read his books and felt we had to respond. He was describing the generation slightly older than ours, but it was similar to our generation.*

On the Road *was about American travel. John and Tommy began hitch-hiking around the U.S.A. around the same time that we were all reading Kerouac. Maybe they were thinking they were like Kerouac's Sal Paradise and Dean Moriority. John also wrote stories of his travels. Kerouac's call to the road was a response to the doldrums, an escape from the strain with parents, a search for what life was about—hit the road, hitch-hike, and find out. Kerouac wrote, "Somewhere along the line I knew there'd be girls, visions, everything; somewhere along the line the pearl would be handed to me."*

I was restrained from joining my friends on the road by my retired nature and also the sword over my head known as the Naval Reserve. I had to be there at the Navy meeting every Tuesday night.

Tommy Oakland was the wildest of my intimate friends, and he had become somewhat of an on-the-roader even before Kerouac. The beat writing helped to direct him. When he would come to our house, he would be loud and like a jumping jack. You could even hear him shouting to himself half a block away before he reached us. He was something like Dean in On the Road, *and I was something like Sal who said, "All my other current friends were 'intellectuals' . . . but Dean just raced in society, eager for bread and love, he didn't care one way or another . . . "*

Although I did not travel, I imbibed the Kerouac doctrine. I liked the way he wrote:

> *The only people for me are the mad ones, the ones who are mad to live, mad to talk, mad to be saved, desirous of everything at the same time, the ones who never yawn or say the commonplace thing, but burn, burn, burn like fabulous yellow Roman candles. . . .*

Almost everyone in his book was part of one loose gang or family. His friends were always meeting up with one another, traveling all the way from San Francisco to the East Coast and suddenly showing up at your house. The one thing they all had in common was that they were all searching. And belief in God was part of it, "And of course, no one can tell us that there is no God. We've passed through all forms . . . Everything is fine, God exists without qualms."

The book went from East Coast to West, hitch-hiking, making out sometimes with girls, getting drunk and high and talking in visions, and road and law problems. Kerouac described himself as a "strange, solitary, crazy, Catholic mystic." He was extravagant, unlike me, but he was a writer, and he hinted that there might be an American sainthood, a new religion, but it would have to be found in a free way, by wandering and living a wild and rhapsodic life, "desiring everything at once." I couldn't keep up the pace, but some of it got into my blood. I thought, "Maybe some day."

If Dr. Alexander was slightly condescending to Catcher in the Rye, *she was outright put off by the "juvenile excesses" of the beat bop artist. I didn't let the disagreement come between us, but neither could I give up my youthful yes-saying to Jackie Kero-wacky.*

Anything I say now, over thirty years later, about *On The Road* can be held against me on the grounds that I am an old man—a monk too—talking about youth. But I am not just talking from my present age of fifty. I joined Śrīla Prabhupāda's spiritual family when I was twenty-six years old, and as a *sannyāsī,* I have had more than ample opportunity to fulfill any wanderlust I caught from *On The Road.*

The *sannyāsī's* life has always been one of freely traveling. A *sannyāsī* is not supposed to stay in any place more than three days. Śrīla Prabhupāda told us that there is even a class of *sannyāsīs* who keep in perpetual movement as a symbol of their renunciation. When Lord Caitanya traveled on foot for six years throughout South India, He had a purpose—

to visit pilgrimage sites and to deliver whomever He met into Kṛṣṇa consciousness. Although He had His mission, one gets a sense by reading *Caitanya-caritāmṛta,* that the Lord had great freedom to go wherever he liked. Similarly, Nārada Muni traveled from one planet to another very freely. And Śrīla Prabhupāda often describes Nārada as "traveling without any engagement." There is also a story from the life of St. Francis of Assisi, who walked with a companion. When they came to a crossroads, Francis asked his companion to spin around and around. Then he suddenly asked him to stop—wherever he was pointed, they went in that direction, for preaching.

Kerouac's traveling, although it was searching, was mostly searching without finding. Many boys who came to Śrīla Prabhupāda to become his disciples, had similar kinds of wanderlust. Prabhupāda said that it had to be dovetailed in the service of Kṛṣṇa or else it was useless touring:

> I can understand you are planning to go on world tour, but I think there is no need for wasting your time on such world tour. Better you chant Hare Krishna sitting in one place, that is far better. What for you want to go on world tour—people everywhere are doing the same thing, eating, sleeping, mating and defending—each in some slightly different way, but same substance is there. There are the same streets, same people, same cars, same trees, etc., everywhere, somewhere a hill, somewhere sandy, somewhere some water—but what is the profit of seeing so much scenery? It is better if you want to travel, you can

> travel to preach and spread this Krishna Consciousness to the suffering humanity at large. You can travel with our samkirtana party if you like. They are presently here in Los Angeles, and they are making program to go to London, and then over Europe, then eventually on to India, etc. So if you want to travel, I recommend you travel with them, and chant Hare Krishna with them wherever you go. And you will profit by this sort of travel, whereas the other is a waste of time practically. . . .
>
> —Letter of November 13, 1968

I have written my own *Lessons From the Road,* which combines travel writing similar to travel writers like Kerouac, with the spiritual vision given to me by Śrīla Prabhupāda.

> It is the duty of a mendicant *(parivrājakācārya)* to experience all varieties of God's creation by traveling alone through all forests, hills, towns, villages, etc., to gain faith in God and strength of mind as well as to enlighten the inhabitants with the message of God.
>
> —*Bhāg.* 1.6.13, purport

I do not agree with Kerouac's philosophy of "burn, burn, burn." If you burn up the adrenalin without any transcendental guidance, you will eventually burn out (as Kerouac did after forty-seven years). We have to first reach the spiritual energy, and then we can become "madmen." There is a kind of renounced *sannyāsī* in Vedic culture known as *avadhūta,* who acts freely without any regard for social conventions. The Six Gosvāmīs of

Vṛndāvana are also described as wandering like madmen on the banks of the Yamunā, calling out, "Where is Kṛṣṇa, where is Kṛṣṇa?" But to become a madman before you are purified means inebrieties and crack-up.

VII

Look Homeward, Angel

When I was seventeen years old, I started keeping a diary, writing in blue ink with an Esterbrook fountain pen. I came home from beer drinking and sat up in bed writing before going to sleep. As I spoke in my diary to Holden Caulfield, I also entered the name of Eugene Gant. That is the name Thomas Wolfe gave to his character in Look Homeward, Angel. *Probably the book was recommended to me by my sister.*

Eugene Gant was the personification of growing up, being sensitive, and wanting to be an artist. Through the medium of Thomas Wolfe, I could discuss these sensitive matters with other friends. Without this medium, I had no other way to interpret my own inner yearnings. I accepted Eugene Gant as my mouthpiece.

One time, I was sitting in a bar filled mostly with college people my age and older, somewhere in Manhattan. A girl sat next to me, and within a few minutes, I mentioned Thomas Wolfe. She replied, "I think he's self-indulgent." I took her remark personally, as if she were criticizing me or my religion. So I defended "my" Thomas Wolfe.

I knew that Wolfe had his critics in the literary world, and he also had his defenders. Some said that he was naive and ignorant of how to write because he wrote so wildly and unmanageably. Thomas Wolfe added to the legend of being an uncontrolled genius by saying that he wrote like "burning lava from a volcano." Others praised him as beyond any equal.

One time I was talking with my college friend Murray, and I approached the subject of Thomas Wolfe. Murray said that the mystery writer, Mickey Spillane, had said about Thomas Wolfe, "He doesn't know what he is doing." To this I replied, "But isn't the unknown the greatest question of all? And isn't life unknown? So the fact that Wolfe doesn't know what he's doing, the fact that he takes life as nameless and lost and unknown, is actually everyone's *position. Those who claim that they* know, *actually are not going deep enough." Murray accepted my defense of Wolfe and said, "Yes, in that sense, he is a great writer." As far as I was concerned, no other sense was worthwhile.*

> . . . A stone, a leaf, an unfound door; of a stone, a leaf, a door. And of all the forgotten faces.
>
> Naked and alone we came into exile. In her dark womb we did not know our mother's face; from the prison of her flesh have we come into the unspeakable and incommunicable prison of this earth.
>
> Which of us has known his brother, which of us has looked into his father's heart? Which of us has not remained forever prison-pent? Which is not forever a stranger and alone?

Whether literary history judges Thomas Wolfe as great or as unmanageable is not important here. I mention him as an item of early love. It is not always easy to recognize how much I was posing in my "love" for Wolfe. First of all, we would have to decide how much Wolfe himself was posing, and *then* how much I was posing. Posing *was* involved, I have no doubt. Even at the time I first read him, I knew that I was posing, but I thought, "Better some pretention of having a soul, than not to have a soul at all." Better to be alive to poetry and idealistic visions, than to be a typical sold-out Staten Island commuter.

One of the scenes in the book I found most moving was the death of Eugene Gant's brother, Ben. When Ben was dying, Eugene was not satisfied to think of the philosophies he had heard in his college class, Descarte, Hegel, and so on. But he turned to prayer. Eugene said, "We can believe in the nothingness of life, we can believe in the nothingness of death and of life after death—but who can believe in the nothingness of Ben?" Eugene visited the grave of his brother and went through a meditation on whether his brother would actually return or live on in some way. On the one hand, he is convinced that, "We shall not come again." But then he thought we would.

> The laurel, the lizard, and the stone will come no more. The women weeping at the gate have gone and will not come again. And pain and pride and death will pass, and will not come again. And light and dawn will pass, and the star and the

> cry of a lark will pass, and will not come again. And we shall pass, and shall not come again.
>
> What things will come again? O Spring, the coolest and fairest of the seasons, will come again. And the strange and varied men will come again, in flower and leaf, the strange and varied men will come again, and death and the dust will never come again, for death and the dust will die. And Ben will come again, he will not die again, in flower and leaf, in wind and music far, he will come back again.
>
> O Lost, and by the wind grieved, ghost, come back again!

What young man could not be moved by these chants and intonations?

I did not so much like the portraits of the Gant family members and relatives, but Eugene's view of the universe was good to read. At the end of the book, although he is still a young man, he desires to escape the confines of his mother's house, but he is still attached. This sentiment was close to my own mentality when I read Wolfe. He described looking at his mother in the house and hearing a voice within him, the voice of life, telling him that it is time now to leave, grow up, go into the world on his own. The young boy within Eugene engages in a dialogue with the voice within him:

> (You are alone now, it said. You must escape, or you will die.) It is all like death, she fed me at her breasts, I slept in the same bed with her, she took me on her trips. All of that is over now, and each time it was like a death. (And like a life, it said to him, each time that you die, you will be

> born again. And you will die a hundred times before you become a man.) I can't! I can't! Not now—later, more slowly. (No. Now, it said.) I'm afraid. I have nowhere to go. (You must find a place, it said.) I am lost. (You must hunt for yourself, it said.) I am alone. Where are you? (You must find me, it said.)

Wolfe's theme of the lostness of life was poignant but vague to me: Whatever happens in life is then lost forever. We live here, and especially when we are young, we don't know who we are or who our father and mother are, and in any case, everything is lost too soon and never to return. More simply and plainly, I was drawn to the theme of growing up and some day leaving Mom and Dad and 125 Katan Avenue. Wolfe became my friend and poet guide.

Now I am more demanding than I was in my youth when I first read Wolfe. I must ask, "What is the foundation of his philosophy?" One of Wolfe's critics at the time he was writing said that he did not employ enough art and that "genius" is not enough. But we may say to the literary critics that art is also not enough. For one to be a teacher and an artist or even a real human being, he must find out the absolute truth. The writer especially needs to know this. In a sense, the writer is like the guru for humankind, and as it is said in Vedic literature, "One should not become a guru unless he can deliver his followers from death." A writer's main concern is to portray life, but once we start to write of life, that leads us to ultimate questions. If we try to describe life without knowing the ultimate truth, then we stop short and just go on making rhetoric without enlightenment. We express anguish and joy, but with no revelation or solution. There is ultimately no release.

The writer who is not on the path of the absolute truth describes ultimate problems of existence only as a kind of fiction. Thus, at the end of *Angel,* we have a fictional scene of Eugene with the ghost of his dead brother Ben, conversing about many topics such as whether there is life after death. At best it is a poetic device and we may flow with it in order to speculate along with Wolfe on the meaning of existence.

My intention here is not to put down my old heroes, but the truth has to be stated. We have every right to demand this truth of the books that we read. By their enchanting art, and their genuine evocations, the writers make us their followers. In return, they are obliged to lead us—and not in circles or into a ditch.

There have been many seminars and papers and books about the meaning of Thomas Wolfe's books. Sometimes scholars discuss whether Wolfe believed in a previous existence as did the poet Wordsworth. Did he believe in God? What does he actually mean by the ghost and the angel? What does he mean when he says that the ultimate meaning of life is to reconcile yourself with your father? What is behind all the rhetoric? The scholars discuss these things but come up with no definite conclusions, because Wolfe himself was not writing clearly. The scholars speculate, but no one knows.

A person may think that there is life after death. Another may think that we do not return. And someone else may say that we return, but only as the material elements. But for such an inconceivable subject, our intuitions and feelings in the night, however powerful they may be, cannot constitute shared knowledge. Therefore, the Vedic process is to find out the meaning of existence by approaching authorized sources of knowledge, transcendental scripture and realized persons. If this can be done by aspiring writers and geniuses, then the day will come when the West will be blessed with artists who can write of real life, and at the same time, give enlightenment, ultimate knowledge. That will give true help and guidance to hungry young souls, and not just leave them with memories that fade.

VIII

Reading on the Job

For the two summers that I was in junior college, I worked for the Parks Department at Great Kills Beach on Staten Island. The pay wasn't terrific, but it wasn't a hard-working job. You got to hang around the beach. I was also able to read a lot while at work. I used to sit on a bench near the bath house and collect tickets. When people came by I would look up, and they would give me a ticket and show me their key. But mostly I could read, and the bosses didn't mind when they went by and saw me reading.

I liked to impress people with what I was reading. "Parkies" wore green t-shirts and orange pants, so I would keep a book in my back pocket, ready to read whenever I could. I also liked to have the title sticking out to impress people. During this time I was reading Neitzsche. I also had a book about him by the scholar, Walter Kauffman. I couldn't understand Neitzsche very well, and Kauffman was making it clear to me, so I had both in my pocket. We parkies were hanging around at the counter where people bought hotdogs and sodas. One girl came alone who was a fellow student in the community college. She noticed the book, saying in a pleasant way, "Oh, you're reading Neitzsche." That was cal-

culated; she was supposed to notice. Another time, I was in the parking lot showing people where to park, and the title of the book was showing in my pocket. It was Oscar Wilde. Someone came by and said, "Oh, you're reading Oscar Wilde?" I also read a popular book that I thought was funny, No Time for Sargeants. *I sat on my chair and laughed out loud.*

One summer I concentrated on Dostoyevsky. I perched the chair at a little angle against the bath house wall, and sat and read. One rainy day, no one came to the beach, and so I read The Brothers Karamazov *all day. What is life? What is God? One of Dostoevsky's main themes was the existence of God, not in a theological tract way, but God in people's lives. And crime. People committing crimes, being sinful; people trying to repent and get God's grace. That is one of the themes he studies over and over again in a novel like* Crime and Punishment. *Karamazov is a murderer; in* The Idiot, *there is also a murder. People going to prison and seeking resolution for their sins through Jesus Christ or through a monk; real, passionate people.*

On rainy days, I could read all morning, take a break for lunch, and then get back to my book. Just read the whole day.

On one overcast day, I read the dialogues of Plato and paid close attention to Socrates' argument for the eternality of the soul. I followed his logic and was convinced.

In his introduction to *The Brothers Karamazov*, Dostoevsky writes as follows: "The main question that will be discussed in all the parts is one that has worried me, consciously or unconsciously, all my life—the existence of God. During his life, my character is at times an atheist, at times a believer, a fanatic, a dissenter, and again an atheist. The second story will take place in a monastery. I put all my hopes in the second story. Perhaps people will at last say that not everything I have written is a lot of nonsense."

Recalling my summertime reading into God consciousness makes me wonder, "Was I at any time God conscious before I met Śrīla Prabhupāda, or was I even close to it?" In one sense, I was not even close. The Vedic mantra states, "*oṁ ajñana timirāndhāsya* . . . I was standing in darkness with my eyes shut, and my spiritual master came and forced open my eyes with the torchlight of transcendental knowledge. Therefore, I offer my respectful obeisances to him." But we are also informed that Lord Kṛṣṇa is always present everywhere. When I finally met Śrīla Prabhupāda and began reading *Bhagavad-gītā*, then for the first time, I learned that *all of us have always been Kṛṣṇa conscious living entities.* "Kṛṣṇa consciousness is not an artificial imposition on the mind. It is the original energy of the self." So the enlightenment that Śrīla Prabhupāda gave us throws light not only on our present and future, but upon our past.

Bhagavad-gītā teaches that the very existence of consciousness is a kind of proof of spiritual existence. Lord Kṛṣṇa says, "That which pervades the entire body you should know to be indestructible."

And Śrīla Prabhupāda comments, "This verse more clearly explains the real nature of the soul, which is spread all over the body. Anyone can understand what is spread all over the body: it is consciousness" (*Bg.* 2.17, purport). We say, "My hand," "my head," but who am I? These are basic ways to meditate upon consciousness and the self. And human consciousness, being particularly developed, is intended for God consciousness.

When during a slow day at Great Kills Park, I read about the existence of God in Socrates and Dostoevsky, that was a further development of consciousness. But whether I remained undeveloped or developed in consciousness, the elemental *existence* of consciousness was a fact I could sometimes perceive. Although I cannot recall the details, I think there were little moments when this awareness dawned on me. Even in earliest childhood I sometimes became aware, "This is me, I am here." And now recalling the books in my life, I also relive an awareness, "Yes, that was me. I was there in the past, just as I exist now and I will exist in the future." I know it is stretching the point to say that I was God conscious before I met Śrīla Prabhupāda. These moments do not have a direct Kṛṣṇa conscious content, although they may be early phases of awareness. If I had never met a pure devotee of the Lord, then my excursions into God conscious reading or an occasional awareness of my existence, would not have added up to much. But now I can see these things for what they were. Consciousness plus Kṛṣṇa equals Kṛṣṇa consciousness. And Kṛṣṇa consciousness is always awakened by association with the pure devotees of Lord Kṛṣṇa.

It is also the nature of eclectic reading, that sometimes you read high and sometimes you read low. One day you are deeply into Socrates, and then you are guffawing over the slapstick in *No Time for Sargeants.* On a rainy day, you may sit alone furrowing your brow and considering immortality, but when the sun comes out, you are hanging around the hotdog stand, showing off in front of the girls. You read and read and read, but it doesn't seem to add up. I remember once being introduced by a friend who said of me, "He's got a big backlog of novels." At first I couldn't understand what he meant. A backlog of novels? He said, "I mean, you have read a lot." It was true that my reading was starting to accumulate. I had read many Charles Dickens novels and big volumes of Dostoevsky and all of Marcel Proust. But it really didn't seem to make me any happier, this big backlog. The predicament of the eclectic reader is also described by Kṛṣṇadāsa Kavirāja in *Caitanya-caritāmṛta:*

> If one becomes a bookworm, reading many books and scriptures and hearing many commentaries and the instructions of many men, this will produce doubt within his heart. One cannot in this way ascertain the real goal of life.
>
> —*Cc. Ādi* 16.11

This verse occurs as a description of Tapana Miśra, a learned scholar who met Lord Caitanya. Elaborating on the point, Śrīla Prabhupāda writes,

"In this connection, Śrīla Bhaktisiddhānta Sarasvatī Ṭhākura gives his opinion that those who are attracted to studying many kinds of literature concerning various subject matters, especially fruitive activities and philosophical speculation, are deprived of unalloyed devotional service because of their splayed attention. . . . Lord Caitanya's instruction to Tapana Miśra is especially significant for persons who loiter here and there collecting books and reading none of them, thus becoming bewildered regarding the aim of life."

All I can say is, thank God I met Śrīla Prabhupāda. Otherwise, my life might be summed up with an epitaph, "He has a big backlog of novels" (to which a *brahmacārī* might reply, "So what? He missed the real point of life, didn't he?"). Yes, his books were the burden that drowned him. He read but never learned to swim.

IX

Neitzsche

One day while browsing in the Eighth Street bookstore in Manhattan, I picked up a Modern Library Giant, several volumes in one, the philosophy of Fredrick Neitzsche. It had a black dust jacket with some gold, and a silhouette of him with his big mustache. I don't know why I bought it; it was extra-curricular reading. His name was often dropped by intellectuals, and I was eager to read his poetic work, Thus Spake Zarathustra. *You would browse in the bookstore and something would hit you, and you would say, "I think it's time for me to get this."*

Neitzsche is remembered as the philosopher who declared, "God is dead." He challenged the whole Western civilization and institution of Christianity. He was a loner, glorifying the individual. I remember him saying about himself, "I am like a solitary pine tree on a tall mountain."

I carried the Modern Library Giant of Neitzsche home, and as soon as I entered the living room, my father saw the big book. "What's that?" he asked. He took one look at it and didn't like it. I had, of course, reached the stage where I could read books without showing them to him for approval, but he gave his opinion anyway. He said, "From what I've heard about him, nobody can under-

stand his philosophy. What he has written is not even coherent. And the Nazis claim they were influenced by him. I don't think there is any good in your reading it. I don't know why you got it. You better watch yourself. He could really mess you up."

I didn't appreciate comments like this from my father. I thought, "Boy, Dad is so ignorant that he doesn't know about Neitzsche. He never read him, maybe just something in the New York Daily News. *He's not at all qualified to say." I wouldn't say all that, but I said, "No Dad, it's not like that. He is actually considered one of the great philosophers in Western literature." Then my father might say something like, "I think they're all misfit bastards." He would look out the window as he said it, and then walk into the kitchen.*

I did not study Neitzsche under a teacher in a philosophy course, but on my own, as an impressionable teenager. The special book for me was *Thus Spake Zarathustra.* I became intoxicated by its poetry and aphorisms. Although I was not able to grasp from it a consistent or clear philosophy, I was knocked over by one-liners like, "Of all writings, I love only that which is written with blood." Even if I had only fifteen minutes at night before going to sleep, I would open the book and ingest a few pages, each written with the greatest intensity. As Neitzsche said, "I have at all time written my writings with my whole heart and soul. I do not know what purely intellectual problems are."

Years later I read critical studies of his work and began to piece together the system he was propounding, but by then, the ardor was gone.

And that was the best thing about Neitzsche for me, not so much what he was saying, but his passion for intellectual life. I read him at a time when my own intellectual life was just erupting. My "eruption" was a minor one, but his was like the blowing up of the Earth. Even my fired-up professors were not this hot! Neitzsche's claim, which I tended to believe, was that he *lived and felt* ideas as no one before him had done: "I speak only of things I have *experienced* and do not offer only events in the head. One must want to experience the great problems with one's body and one's soul."

Although I was not sophisticated enough to follow this heavy-weight philosopher step-by-step, I did receive the message of skepticism:

> God is dead. God remains dead. And we have killed Him. How shall we, the murderer of all murderers, console? That which was holiest and mightiest of all that the world has yet possessed has bled to death under our knives—who will wipe this blood off us? With what water could we purify ourselves? What festivals of atonement, what sacred game shall we need to invent? Is not the greatness of this deed too great for us? Must we not ourselves become God just to seem worthy of it? There has never been a greater deed—and whoever shall be born after us for the sake of this deed, he shall be a higher history than all history hitherto.

And so I duly informed the priests of St. Clare's church, by a note under the door, of what Neitzsche had said.

But sometimes he seemed not at all skeptical, as if he were writing according to changing moods or growth. Therefore, he was sometimes negative and sometimes hopeful. Was he saying that all skepticism was actually leading up to a new, grander affirmation?

> All our great teachers and predecessors have at last come to a stop. . . . It will be the same with you and me! But what does that matter to you and me! *Other birds will fly farther!* . . . Will it perhaps be said of us that we too, *steering westward* hoped to reach an India, but that it was our fate to be wrecked against infinity?

Gradually I began to at least recognize his main slogans or themes. The Superman, the will to the Superman, the will to power and self-overcoming. Live dangerously! Eternal recurrence. Total affirmation of life. The great noontide. It was a new, prophetic language apparently invented by Neitzsche himself. But his claim was that he was expressing the ultimate truth.

The section of *Zarathustra* that I loved the most, and which I reread to myself and read to my friends was "The Song of Yes and Amen":

> The world is deep,
> deeper than they can comprehend.
> Deep is its woe,
> joy—deeper than heart's agony:

Woe says: Fade! Go!
But all joy wants eternity—
wants deep, deep, deep eternity!

I cannot remember a poem gripping me as much as this one. All joys want eternity, want deep, deep eternity. And then Zarathustra said, "Never yet did I find a woman by whom I wanted children, unless it be this woman whom I love: For I love you, O Eternity. *For I love you, O Eternity!"* And then paragraph after paragraph ended with the refrain, *"For I love you, O Eternity."* Believing in his earnestness, I knew that eternity was not just an idea for this philosopher, *but it mattered.* He was lamenting over the fact that nothing in the world was eternal. As I read, I myself became concerned. I did not know what I was going to do about *my life* or what the consequences were to my sharing Neitzsche's concern for eternity. But share it I did. At least while reading alone in my room, I thought that eternity was the most important of all things.

My reminiscence of *Zarathustra* is in no way an attempt to assess Neitzsche's work. His thought is deep and hard to grasp, and I am only telling my youthful impressions. But since I have started it, let me continue to tell how I fared with Neitzsche over the years. I continued to be an "official" follower of his and sometimes reread him or spoke up on his behalf. One memory is an exchange I had about Neitzsche when I went into active service in the Navy. I will jump ahead in my narrative just to tell it.

On board the ship U.S.S. Saratoga, among all the uncultured sailors, I managed to meet one friend who had a keen interest in Zen Buddhism. In order to share with him one of my favorite books, I lent him my copy of *Thus Spake Zarathustra.* My friend read some of it and was not impressed. "Too much wind," he said. He commented that the great philosopher was like a big sailing ship puffed-up with his own wind. On the one hand, I was hurt by this remark, but I immediately saw his point and had to admit that Neitzsche was too much under his own steam. The Zen that I was sharing with my friend was so much different—it was not manmade grandeur, not even the grandeur of the greatest individual intellect straining to know everything; too much wind.

I continued to read *Zarathustra* even in the years after the Navy, and I recall being on a lunch break from a part-time job on Chambers Street, Manhattan, sitting on the courthouse steps, reading and thinking about the Will to Power. I liked Neitzsche's odes to asceticism, solitude, and individuality, but there was something to the Will to Power (as far as I could understand it) that I found unattractive. Sometimes I was tired of how he was always smashing, smashing.

As time went by, *Zarathustra* became harder to return to because I became more aware that he was a fiction. There actually was no person Zarathustra living on a mountain and deciding to come down and teach his doctrine to humankind. This Superman was Neitzsche's invention, and Neitzsche himself was a most tragic human being. I did not want to cheaply attack him, as my dad might, by saying, "If he was such a great philosopher, how come he went crazy?" And yet it frightened me to think that Neitzsche ended his life insane, in a condition of mental and physical paralysis. They said his disease probably came from syphillis, but it also seemed that he went mad because he dared to face the abyss and the riddle to life as no human being had ever dared. He was brave, but was destroyed by forces beyond him. Although I sympathized with his "martyrdom," I wondered if there was a better way.

Since I have brought the momentous subject of Neitzsche thus far, I feel compelled to make comments from the Kṛṣṇa conscious viewpoint. An analysis of Neitzsche's thought by a devotee will have to be done in the future by one trained in Western philosophy. But this much I know:

tarko 'pratiṣṭhaḥ śrutayo vibhinnā
nāsāv ṛṣir yasya mataṁ na bhinnam
dharmasya tattvaṁ nihitam guhāyām
mahājano yena gataḥ sa panthāḥ

Dry arguments are inconclusive. A great personality whose opinion does not differ from others is not considered a great sage. Simply by studying the *Vedas,* which are variegated, one cannot come to the right path by which religious principles are understood. The solid truth of religious principles is hidden in the heart of an unadulterated self-realized person. Consequently, as the *śāstras*

> confirm, one should accept whatever progressive path the *mahājanas* advocate.
>
> —*Mahābharata, Vana-parva,* 313.117

One great philosopher is replaced by another. This was exactly the approach of Neitzsche who claimed that no one in the thousands of years of history before him had thought so powerfully and originally. But now scholars and philosophers regularly dissect Neitzsche's philosophy and find it faulty in many ways. So the warning is given in the *Mahābharata* verse, that if you follow one philosopher, eventually new logicians will come to dismantle what your teacher has said. The fact that your favorite philosopher constructed his own view of the universe by mental speculation, opens it up to further speculation by other individuals. But those who follow the unbroken disciplic succession of Vedic thought, based on the *śruti* or revealed wisdom, keep consistent and free from the faults of mental speculation. Of course, the mental speculators will attack the Vedic *paramparā,* but the devotee-scholars remain intact, and their accumulated commentaries preserve the Vedic culture for those who in every age want to seek relief from mental speculation. One who actually wants to know the source of everything and the purpose of human life, can find shelter in the unbroken disciplic succession of Vedic knowledge, which is never changed by the fashionable trends of passing centuries, or subject to demolition by high-powered speculators, who themselves come and go. Even when there *is* a need to emphasize a particular *dharma* for the age, it can be drawn from the Vedic literature, as was done by Lord Caitanya, without any speculation or minimization of Vedic authority.

Neitzsche's famous demolition of "God" seemed to me, even when I read it, more of an attack on Christendom. By attacking the Biblical God, he also attacked all theism, and yet he did not really address the scientific presentation of *Vedānta-sūtra* and *Śrīmad-Bhāgavatam.* The Vedic *ācāryas* have plenty to say about Neitzsche's speculation. Although Neitzsche is hard to pin down because of his personal evolution and his freedom to contradict himself, he also seemed to mostly be saying that the God who is worshiped in the West is one who has died. In other words, a civilization built on the simplistic worship of God, as well as the corruption caused by deviant claims to worship God, as well as the earlier piety—all of these have died. But God, if truly defined, is one who cannot die.

Śrīla Prabhupāda used to give an analogy about this. He said that if a man goes to a doctor and the doctor finds the man in good health, his circulation, heartbeat, and all other living symptoms nicely operating—if the doctor still concludes, "Sir, you are dead"—that is certainly a crazy analysis. Similarly, since we find the universe operating with great precision and potency, the sun rising daily and orbiting, all the planets orbiting around the sun, and all species of life coming forth and disappearing, how can one say that the universe has no life? A "God" invented by man may be destroyed by him; but the real God is the source of everyone. He is not subject to the petty attacks of speculators or Neitzsche's rhetorical men with knives. Neitzsche claimed that now that they have killed God, they themselves will become God, but this is only crazy talk. The gods continue to come and go like specks of straw in the sea. When the pure devotee of God comes into the world, he himself proves that God lives, and therefore, the *Mahābharata* advises us, *mahājano yena gataḥ sa panthāḥ:* Follow the *mahājanas.*

When Śrīla Prabhupāda first came to the Lower East Side in 1966, the underground newspaper, *East Village Other,* printed an article in which they parodied the aphorism, "God is dead." The writer told a story that once there was a group of theologians who had killed an old man in a church and subsequently, the press report came out that God was now dead. But some people didn't believe it. They had dug up the body and found it to be "not the body of God, but that of his P.R. men: organized religion." At once, the good tidings swept across the world: "GOD LIVES! . . . But where was God?"

> A full-page ad in *The New York Times,* offering a reward for information leading to the discovery of the whereabouts of God, and signed by Martin Luther King and Ronald Reagan, brought no response. People began to worry and wonder again. "God," said some people, "lives in a sugar cube." Others whispered that the sacred secret was in a cigarette.
>
> But while all this was going on, an old man, one year passed his allotted three score and ten,

wandered into New York's East Village and set about to prove to the world he knew where God could be found. In only three months, the man, Swami A.C. Bhaktivedanta, succeeded in convincing the world's toughest audience—Bohemians, acid-heads, pot-heads, and hippies—that he knew the way to God: Turn Off, Sing Out, and Fall In. This new brand of holy man, with all due deference to Dr. Leary, has come forth with a brand of "Consciousness Expansion" that's sweeter than acid, cheaper than pot, and nonbustable by fuzz. How is all this possible? "Through Krishna," the Swami says.

—*Śrīla Prabhupāda-līlāmṛta,* Volume 2, pp. 221-22

Neitzsche was one of the writers I had in mind when I asked Śrīla Prabhupāda, "What about the God consciousness of the great Western thinkers?" I would have found it very difficult to simply dismiss Neitzsche as a rascal or demon. And Prabhupāda did not ask me to do that. He said that their *sincerity* was their God consciousness. And so I may continue to thank Neitzsche for the poem, "For I love you, O Eternity!" Now that Śrīla Prabhupāda has introduced me to the Supreme Personality of Godhead, Śrī Kṛṣṇa, there is another line of Neitzsche that takes on a delightful meaning: "I should believe only in a God who understood how to dance."

3

Bachelor of Arts

I

Learning With a Teacher

By the time I transferred to Brooklyn college, most of my courses were in my major, English literature. I took a course in American literature with the department chairman, Professor Lewis Solomon. He was a very proper person with gray suits, a dignified mustache, and a deep voice with careful diction. One day, he asked the class for our impressions of Walt Whitman. I raised my hand and said, "He's more than a poet, he's like a prophet." This was the side of Whitman that I was attracted to. I was posing as someone who had something interesting to say about poets and prophets. I always had mixed motives when I spoke in class.

Professor Solomon's class was interesting, but I got the impression that he had done this year after year, the same syllabus, the same authors, in the same way. Although he had an interest in the literature, he wasn't blazing away. Dr. Alexander and Dr. Pessen had more spontaneity. Solomon seemed like he was listening to the sound of his voice, because it was such a deep, perfectly modulated voice. But it was good and new to me; it wasn't the hundredth time I was hearing it. I wanted to get a scholarly understanding of these American writers, so I was interested.

I once went to see Professor Solomon in his office. He had been discussing two schools of literature, Naturalism and Realism. I couldn't quite understand the difference. I decided to go and ask him this question. He gave me an appointment. It must have been a botheration, because he was such a busy person as the chairman of the English department. He explained to me that in Realism, the writers try to describe daily life exactly as it is, as far as they can do it. Naturalism, however, is a school in which they don't just take life as it is, but focus on the sores and the gutter and the suffering. It is more of a turning of the camera to focus on the "human condition" up close. After he explained it, I said thank you. It was such a small exchange and filled with so much ambivalence—perhaps my question was not intelligent, maybe I was bothering him, or maybe he thought I was just posing as a dedicated student. It was hardly like going to see a guru and walking away with your life changed. It was just a small, scholarly point that had to be clarified.

I do not want to knock over the figures in my past as if they were bowling pins. It would be too easy: I could say Solomon was bored teaching American literature, whereas a devotee of Kṛṣṇa is thrilled at every moment, despite repeated readings of the same *Bhagavad-gītā*. Or I could say that as a college student, I studied poetry mostly to get an "A," whereas in Kṛṣṇa consciousness, I serve my guru simply to please him. Or, when I went for a personal meeting with my English teacher, it was dry and didn't inspire me to change in any way, whereas in one eleventh of a second in my Guru Mahārāja's presence, I taste liberation. But the truth is not that completely black and white, and imperfections continue to exist even in spiritual relationships, at least from the viewpoint of the neophyte disciple.

There is a vast difference between material and spiritual life, and I am grateful to know it. Thank God I didn't have to decide, "I guess I will try to become like Professor Solomon. I can't think of any alternative for a career." Imagine teaching year after year, Whitman and Dickenson, Thoreau and Emerson, Poe and Hawthorne, Naturalism and Realism. Aside from the fact that the poets and their writings are limited, it is also the *way* they are studied by the academicians that makes it so mundane. The students read books to get a passing or excelling grade, and the teachers teach poetry according to academic formulas as a means of income. Walt Whitman *was* daring and lyrical, Dickenson was looking intently toward Eternity—whereas Solomon and his students were just fooling around, intellectualizing, drying out life like strips of fish in the sun. And how dry it must become when repeated year after year!

It could be said without much exaggeration that most authors are ruined for students when read within a college course. It is a terrible setting for actual learning. For myself, whatever juice I got from books was mostly done in extra-curricular reading, without the pressure of exams and grades, and without the pressure of exams and grades, and without having to memorize and submit to an "authorized" version of the poet's worth and meaning.

Coming from Staten Island, I wanted to prove myself worthy in the academic big leagues, and so I became a dancing dog. I strived to get all "A's." "Walt Whitman, are you going to stand in the way of my getting an 'A,' or will I be able to conquer you for my purposes? Emily Dickenson, please don't hide your inner life from me, because I have to make clear sense out of you for my final exam."

I don't have much live remembrance of these authors, probably because I studied them within the syllabus of American Literature 101. I know what Emily Dickenson is *supposed* to be—brilliant, transcendental, one of the greatest poets of all time—and I know Whitman has been a direct inspiration for generations of American poets, but for me they remain mangled as school subjects.

Some of this contamination may have carried over into my approach to Śrīla Prabhupāda as his student. But if I thought studying *Bhagavad-gītā* was another academic task to conquer, Śrīla Prabhupāda soon made it clear that knowledge of Kṛṣṇa was not to be achieved by academic striving. You must study *Bhagavad-gītā* by practicing with your whole life. You live with the teacher. He has no private life separate from the classroom. He is qualified by a hundred percent devotion to Lord Kṛṣṇa. He does not come bearing academic credentials and giving you lists of scholarly books to read and suggesting that you too might become a university professor. But he comes in *paramparā* of pure devotee-scholars, and he hints that you can become an ecstatic lover of the all-attractive Personality of Godhead. You sing with him, eat with him, and learn how to spiritualize all your acts. You learn love of God from him and come to love him as your saving guide.

It usually takes time to do all this, more than a fraction of a second, but at every step, it is solid and real and progressive. You are not just another face in the class for only one semester, and then gone. He is always your teacher, life after life. And you can't cop a quick "A" from him by cleverly regurgitating what he says on a two-hour exam. He tests you by many practical austerities and menial services. It is hard, it is surrender. But you are convinced that he has seen the truth and he can deliver you from nescience. He has implicit faith in Lord Kṛṣṇa and in his guru, and so he knows the scriptures by revelation. You can know too. By becoming his student, you can solve all the perplexities of life. This is just a small summation of the guru-disciple life. Suffice to say, you will not find it in the university, or even on your own by reading a poet who has not become a disciple of a bona fide guru.

II

The Heart of Hamlet

Professor Grebanier was completely different from Lewis Solomon, whose name describes him. Solomon was a solemn man, whereas Dr. Grebanier was obese and gushing. He reminded me of pictures you see of Dr. Samuel Johnson from the 18th Century. Grebanier was always saying "brilliant," witty things or being insulting. He presented himself as thoroughly realized in all literature and he pontificated on everything.

When I told my Staten Island friend, Tommy Oakland, about Grebanier, Tommy wanted to come and sit in on one of the classes. Tommy was so outgoing that you could hear him laughing and appreciating in the back seat where he was auditing the class. He was practically jumping up in his seat. Grebanier gave quite an electric session.

I took two courses from him, one on poetry and one on Shakespeare. The Shakespeare course was very popular and was held in a large hall that slanted downwards. There were over a hundred students in that class. We used Grebanier's own book called The Heart of Hamlet. *In this book, he blasted all critics of* Hamlet. *Every scholar had some interpretation of* Hamlet, *but he said that they had all completely confused the play. Grebanier's interpretation was like a perverted reflection of what Prabhupāda actually did in the* Bhagavad-gītā As It Is. *Grebanier was saying that only* he *knew* Hamlet *as it is. The trouble with everyone else is that they put their own speculations in and tried to teach their philosophies. They thought that Shakespeare did not even know what he was doing. But actually, the play is very clear. All you have to do is study the texts and you can understand the motivations of Hamlet, why he hesitated to kill his father's murderer, and what he really meant when he said, "To be or not to be." On each and every point there is no need for speculation.*

Grebanier's book was like he himself, filled with witty footnotes and digressions. He caricatured and made fun of all the other scholars. He was convinced of all his own eccentricities and excesses. He was right. What he was saying made the play understandable. So he taught from that book, and it took a long time, going carefully over each line.

One day we came to class, the morning after the presidential election of 1960. President Kennedy had won over Nixon in a very close vote. Almost everyone at Brooklyn College was happy about the result. The day after the election, Eleanor Roosevelt spoke in our Walt Whitman Auditorium and received wild applause. But in Grebanier's class, he was unhappy. He mumbled and muttered, "If that's what the American people want, they are going to be sorry. They think he's good, but he's not." What I didn't know about Grebanier at the time, was that during the McCarthy era, he was a witness who turned in professors as having some alleged connection with the Communist party. This was known to faculty members, and there were professors who would not talk to him or who would leave the room when he entered. I found that out only later.

As far as his being able to teach literature, he was expert. He told us that he also taught poetry in his home for a fee. I never went, but I imagined he had a formal, large apartment with nice furniture. His students would come and sit in chairs, and he would be witty, more relaxed, maybe wearing different clothes, but still as big as a house, and making that funny sound when he laughed.

A Brooklyn College friend of mine wrote a poem about Grebanier calling him, "A ridiculous goose stuffed with opinions." People hearing him had the impression that he was very impressed with his own sparkling remarks, as if he thought they should be remembered for all time, like the aphorisms or witticisms of Samuel Johnson. Grebanier was also the editor of a line of student notes, like Cliff Notes or Student Aids, which gave a rundown of books so students didn't have to read them. I showed one of these booklets to my former professor, Dr. Alexander, and she said, "He's just an entrepreneur."

As I look back, Professor Grebanier's portly form stands in the way of Shakespeare and *Hamlet*. I remember my professor and not the Bard. How little we remember and how strangely it gets filtered down to us! And what does it matter now? As I begin to speak of Grebanier, I am enlivened and amused, but then . . . I have also heard that he has since died. The whole corpulent show is over. No more snickering by him as he puts down the other scholars. And I doubt that his book is used anymore. New "Grebaniers" have come forward, no doubt, to put down his *Heart of Hamlet.*

I do not want to trifle with a sacred cultural monument like *Hamlet*, or its creator. But neither do I want to be sentimental about all this, nor should I simply avoid it. As the saying goes, "If a girl has decided to dance, why is she covering her face with a veil?" Okay, I will tell you what I now think of *Hamlet*.

When I studied it with Grebanier, the big question—which he said puzzled all the inferior scholars—is why did Hamlet hesitate to kill his father's murderer? Everyone had their own opinion about this. Some said that Hamlet was wishy-washy, some said that he did not have sufficient criminal evidence, or that he was too philosophical, and so on. Well, it no longer seems to me to be a deep issue. Even if we get the answer right, whose life will be improved? The questions in the *Śrīmad-Bhāgavatam*, by comparison, are crucial and relevant for everyone's welfare. Mahārāja Parīkṣit's dilemma was, "What is the duty of one who is about to die?" And the question asked by Mahārāja Yudhiṣṭhira (and at another time by Mahārāja Pṛthu) was, "How can we, who are householders and involved in worldly duties, come out of the entanglement of birth and death and achieve spiritual perfection?"

Hamlet asked the question, "To be or not to be?" But he never asked, "Who am I?" He saw the ghost of his father, but he never consulted with a bona fide saintly person who could have raised the issues to the transcendental platform, for everyone's benefit, including those who watch the play. *Hamlet* is tragic, as is all material life. And certainly, Shakespeare spoke like an empowered demigod with abilities for poetic-philosophical expressions that have rarely been equaled. When all is said and done in Act Five, we get a heavy bedload of the dead, but what wisdom? Where is that *Hamlet* where the hero—like Arjuna—is told that he is considering everything on the bodily platform, and that there is a higher truth? Where is that Shakespearean masterpiece where the spirit soul inquires from the guru, "What is my duty?" We want to see that play. That is our demand. *Hamlet* is not transcendental.

When we look at Hamlet from the spiritual perspective (just as when we look at Holden Caulfield) he appears to be a very likely candidate for spiritual knowledge. Consider his famous speech in which he agonized about the temporality of human life:

> I have of late, but wherefore I know not, lost all my mirth, forgone all custom of exercise; and indeed it goes so heavily with my disposition that this goodly frame the earth seems to me a sterile promontory, this most excellent canopy the air, look you, this brave o'erhanging firmament, this majestical roof fretted with golden fire, why, it appeareth nothing to me but a foul and pestilent congregation of vapors. What a piece of work is a

> man, how noble in reason, how infinite in faculties, in form and moving how express and admirable, in action how like an angel, in apprehension how like a god: the beauty of the world, the paragon of animals—and yet, to me, what is this quintessence of dust? Man delights not me—no, not woman neither, though by your smiling you seem to say so.
>
> —*Hamlet,* Act 2, Scene II

Śrīla Prabhupāda says that anyone who comes to the point of seeing that material life is full of perplexities and that it has no real happiness, is advanced in consciousness and is eligible for liberation. Like a god, Shakespeare was able to create characters from all walks of life: kings, soldiers, poets, priests, submissive ladies, ladies of high spirit, buffoons like Falstaff, etc., but where is the knowledgeable guru figure? Where is his Nārada, his Agastya Muni? How wonderful it would be if into the crisis of Shakespeare's tragedies, a guru figure could have walked on stage and resolved things, not from a material point of view, but by showing the real resolution—transcendental knowledge of devotional service to the Supreme.

Of course, we have our playwrights of the spiritual world, especially in Śrīla Rūpa Gosvāmī, and it is not our intention to compare Shakespeare and Rūpa Gosvāmī by literary or artistic analysis. They are worlds apart. My intention is to honestly remember and appreciate my own immersion in Western culture as I grew up, before meeting Śrīla Prabhupāda. But it is inevitable that at least on occasion, we confront the shortcomings of even an empowered bard who lacks that knowledge which descends directly from God through His faithful (*paramparā*) sages.

It may appear that I have said both Grebanier and Śrīla Prabhupāda brought out the truth of the text they studied, while criticizing previous speculations of scholars. But there is a great difference between the two commentators. For one thing, Śrīla Prabhupāda criticized upstart impersonalist speculation of all sorts, but he faithfully represented the disciplic succession of Vaiṣṇava commentators. Prabhupāda never claimed that he was the first one to ever understand the *Bhagavad-gītā.* Furthermore, even if we say that Grebanier removed confusing speculation about *Hamlet* and proved that the play is clear by itself—even then, it is not that *Hamlet*-as-it-is gives us the revealed word of God. When Hamlet's apparently enigmatic motives are actually made clear, then we see him as a conditioned soul who was perhaps not such a big vacillator after all, but who was ignorant of the goal of life and how to achieve it. Thus there is a great difference between allowing Hamlet to speak for himself, and allowing Kṛṣṇa to speak for Himself. When the *Bhagavad-gītā* is cleared from the misconceptions of devious commentators, then the Supreme Lord speaks His loving intentions to all living entities: "Always think of Me, become My devotee, worship Me and offer your homage unto Me. Thus you will come to Me without fail. I promise you this because you are My very dear friend" (*Bg*.18.65). Śrīla Prabhupāda writes, "*Bhagavad-gītā* is not an ordinary book written by a poet or fiction writer; it is spoken by the Supreme Personality of Godhead. Any person fortunate enough to hear these teachings from Kṛṣṇa or from His bona fide spiritual representative is sure to become a liberated person and get out of the darkness of ignorance" (*Bg.* 18.73, purport).

The difference between the Elizabethan playwright and Bhagavān Śrī Kṛṣṇa, is the difference between the finite fallible soul and the infinite Supreme Soul. The benefit that one may derive from reading Kṛṣṇa's words with attention and worship, is also infinitely greater than the benefit of studying Shakespeare's plays.

III

Fathers and Sons in Maya

My father was an anti-intellectual. He called intellectuals egg-heads. Politically, he was a Republican war-hawk. I started subscribing to the Village Voice *while in college and my father didn't like that at all. It was partly because it came from Greenwich Village, but also because the politics were too much for him, the heavy criticism of American foreign policy. I was sympathetic to the black civil rights movement and he was not, but we rarely discussed our differences.*

Aside from the newspaper, my father did not read books. He had one book called As You Pass By. *It was a history of the fire department, starting from when they had horses pull the wagons. It had stories in it like how two different fire companies would get to the fire at the same time and start a fist fight over who would put the fire out, while the house burned down. My father was amused by stories like that. He also used to subscribe to a magazine,* WNYFD (With New York Fire Department). *The best part of that was a gossip column that was divided up into all the different districts and fire houses. It would say things like, "We hear within the Great Kills Station, Lieutenant Jimmy Matthews wasn't very pleased when one of the fire laddies threw a fire cracker into his office . . . Congratulations to Captain Zusekner, whose wife gave birth to baby boys on August 3rd . . ."*

So there was a growing distance between us as I started reading intellectual books, not just as part of the college syllabus, but on my own. One day I came home from classes carrying all my books, and I had a friendly exchange with my father. He was in a good mood and it was a sunny day. As soon as I came into the house, I placed my books down on the table. The book on top was called The Romantic Age, *and it was the textbook for my 19th Century British poetry class. My father looked at it and said, "Oh,* The Romantic Age." *He wanted to make a conversational statement, but said something which showed that he didn't know it was a book of English poetry. He thought it referred to something romantic, olden times. I wasn't annoyed with what he said, but patiently explained what the book actually was. He said nothing further and showed no interest. At least he liked the fact that I was getting good grades in school.*

In my third year at college, I won a twenty-five dollar literary prize. As soon as I received the cash, I went to a bookstore and bought Henry Miller's Tropic of Cancer *and D.H. Lawrence's* Lady Chatterly's Lover. *This was before the breakthroughs in freedom of the press for obscenity. These books were both printed by Grove Press, and they might have been involved in court cases. At this time I was a pseudo-intellectual, snobbish to people who were not intellectual. One just accepted whatever the intellectuals said was good. D.H. Lawrence was supposed to be deep, and his art was considered very good. The fact that he dealt with sexuality and obscenity was not to be considered low class.*

I brought these books into the house covertly. After I read Lady Chatterly's Lover, *I lent it to my sister with a recommendation, "This is a very good book." She was also a pseudo-intellectual.* Lady Chatterly's Lover *began with the line, "Ours is a tragic age and therefore we refuse to take it seriously." That was considered a great line. But then Lawrence got into this love affair between the groundskeeper and an aristocratic lady. A few days later, my sister told me, "Daddy took the book from me." I said, "Wow! How could he do that? That's my book." I was on fire with my new sensibilities, so I went to him and said, "I heard you took the book."*

He responded, "You're damned right I did. You know, if a girl her age reads that book, she'll get all sexed up. I can't have her reading that book."

I said, "Okay, but anyway, I want my book back." It was an intense exchange. I was so righteous, but now that I think of it, he was right. He was right, but I was defending intellectual liberty.

So who was better, the father who didn't know Romantic poetry, or the pseudo-intellectual son? It was all *māyā*—being his son, trying to assert freedom for obscenity, pretending to be a free intellectual, buying books with bright blue dustjackets, turning to the front page, "Ours is a tragic age . . . "

I do not know where my father is now, but he scared the hell out of me the way he forced me to live as he wanted me to be. I was always trying to get away from him one way or another. Living with him was a nightmare. My intellectual pose may have been false, but I was just trying to get out of his clutches. Following Henry Miller seemed to be the way. I liked the way he could write whatever he wanted. He could write "f____" in his books, so he must have been free . . . I am saying *do not* read their books. But also, do not listen to the *māyā* of mothers and fathers who just read their newspapers and their dumb books and watch their TV.

Who do I think I am now, a liberated teacher? No. But I am free of *some* things. I am free of that parental *māyā*. I thank Lord Kṛṣṇa! I am free too, of posing to be a reader of "great books" filled with obscenities. Therefore, I am writing this story hoping it will please those who are also free of these things, and maybe it may help some who are still within the nightmare and don't know how to get out.

I confess that when I go to read the *Śrīmad-Bhāgavatam,* it is not always easy. But I know the *Śrīmad-Bhāgavatam* is beautiful. I have studied it quite a few times. Sometimes it is not easy to read it again, but it is the only book (along with other Vedic literatures) that gives you a direct *darśana* of the Supreme Lord. That is what a book is for. Not for saying, "Ours is a tragic age," or "F____ you." And one reason that we have trouble reading *Śrīmad-Bhāgavatam* is because we have read the other books.

Each person has his or her own karma. Mine was to read many nondevotee books in this lifetime before reading Śrīla Prabhupāda's books. Maybe your karma was to be born of Kṛṣṇa conscious parents and to never read other's speculation or novels. We all have to become lovers of the *Śrīmad-Bhāgavatam,* but not because someone is forcing us. We have to know that there are plenty of books to choose from, yet we still have to decide on Kṛṣṇa.

Life is short. What we read will be on our minds at the time of death. Better it be Kṛṣṇa. We go to the next life according to where our minds are now. At the time of death, we want to think of Kṛṣṇa. We can do it by reading His words now.

Goodbye to the anti-intellectual, the anti-devotee. Even as I write this, and my friend Madhu is talking to Ganga dāsa in the room below,* I keep getting flashes that it is my father's voice down there. But it isn't. He isn't here. I wish him well, wherever he is. But for me, wishing well means "Hare Kṛṣṇa." Father, I send you a God conscious wish. I am a devotee of Śrila Prabhupāda. You hate anything to do with Kṛṣṇa consciousness. I don't know why. The confrontation between us is all over for this lifetime, and I wish you well.

As for this book, obviously I am not writing direct commentary from the *Śrīmad-Bhāgavatam.* I will tell you of the muck and *māyā* I went through, just up to the point of meeting Śrila Prabhupāda. The conclusion is, "All these other books have only glimmers of light, but the full mercy is in *Śrīmad-Bhāgavatam.*"

---

* The sunset is pink, streaking horizontal lines above the clouds over Puffin Island, where I am right now. I am going to tell the others to go out and see it, Kṛṣṇa's picture. The Lord is the greatest artist. Let us take a look. "Up, up my friend and quit your books!" God, it's beautiful!

IV

Steppenwolfe, and Whatever Happened to All the Other Books I Read?

Steppenwolfe *was recommended to me by Dr. Alexander. She probably thought it would appeal to me out of all the books she could have recommended. It was a study of the individual's alienation from bourgeois society. She saw that I was interested in that theme in my reading of modern novels like* On the Road, Catcher in the Rye, *and* Look Homeward, Angel. *I took down the title and the author. This was around 1959-60. I had not heard of Herman Hesse before.*

I went to the Eighth Street bookstore. Nowadays, Steppenwolfe *is a popular paperback, but at that time, it was available only by an obscure publisher in a hardbound volume. The book had a curious, sensual appeal. It was orangish, without a dust jacket, and I was eager to possess it.*

I can no longer remember the story of the novel, but I know it made an impression on me and got into my life. Steppenwolfe *means, "the wolf of the steppes." The main character is a fifty-year old man named Harry. He is an alienated individual with a fantastic dreamy mind, yet he is also attracted to living near the bourgeois world. He writes about how extremely lonely he is, separated from all the ordinary pleasures that mundane persons in society enjoy. One scene I remember—he is sitting on the steps inside the boarding house where he lives. The landlord finds him there and thinks it is rather strange. Then Harry, the Steppenwolfe, asks him to sit beside him. Harry says, "I sit here, but I am looking down at that room on the lower landing. There is such a nice smell of mahogany wood here, and the door to that room looks very clean. The resident has put a plant outside the door in a neat pot, and I can just imagine that inside, everything is kept orderly. It gives me a kind of pleasure to sit here and think of the orderliness of this bourgeois world, as represented in that room. On the other hand, I am completely apart from it, just like a wolf who lives apart from society and cannot expect any society." The picture of his alienation while within the middle-class world struck a chord in me. But Hesse had appreciated what it was like to be a sensitive person, and he illustrated the honest position that such a person must take in relation to the external, material world he lives in.*

Steppenwolfe seems to be gone for me, but when I first read it, it was an exciting new trend. There were always new intellectual fashions to follow, new ways of looking at the universe. People follow the avante-garde philosophers, even if they bring misery, because they are presenting the latest style. "Oh, haven't you heard? We are to feel unhappy by this new philosophy. Man has been defined in a new way, and anybody who is really intelligent is suffering in this way." One trend is replaced by another. In America they tend to cubby-hole these trends by decades, the fifties, the sixties, and so on. In fact, Hesse became popular with the American youth in the sixties.

My love for *Steppenwolfe* may have been pretentious. I liked to think of myself both as a reader of *Steppenwolfe* and as a bit of a Steppenwolfe myself. I remember when I attended the reception for my sister's wedding, I identified with Steppenwolfe there. My father had rented a country club, and everyone was drinking booze and dancing. I had to dance a few times with an aunt, but I was mostly thinking like Harry in *Steppenwolfe*. I was alienated. People were getting drunk and teasing me affectionately, "You're sitting there by yourself, Stevie. Why don't you join the fun?" I had a place of honor at the main table as the bride's brother, but I remained quiet and reserved, as befitting an intellectual poet.

I think I even showed the book to my sister, but that was just the kind of thing that would make her angry with me. "That's what you think you are, you think you are a Steppenwolfe, so you're playing this role that you're so alienated."

There are many other books that I have not mentioned, and to continue to discuss them does not seem relevant. One could discuss any author one likes, but what is the point? A book collector forgets how many books he has kept and where he has kept them all. Some are in his apartment, some are in someone else's apartment, some are left back in his childhood home, or scattered in different places of the world where he has visited. He forgets which books he has not read, and he also gradually forgets the contents of those books he has read. If you ask him about books that were important to him decades ago, he sometimes retains only a summary of how he estimated them in his mind. He may even say that he loves a book, but cannot remember much about it.

He does not want to admit how much he has forgotten, and neither does he want to think that his book-collecting resembles an ordinary hobby like stamp-collecting. Śrīla Prabhupāda compares the speculative book-collector to a donkey carring a staggering burden. The human book-collector is literally like that donkey when he travels—his suitcase, shoulder bags, and cartons have to follow him on the plane and into the taxi.

In the home of the book collector, in addition to the books he has proudly displayed on shelves, his closet spaces and floor spaces are sprawling with volumes. It almost seems like the books, like a rising tide, will gradually edge out the human occupant until there is no more room for him to move or live. He has to keep spending money to buy the latest books and he is also on the mailing list of many publishers who lure him with their titles. He cannot resist seeing or handling new or old books, even though it now becomes clear that he cannot read most of them.

As a bookworm grows older, his memory continues to grow weaker. He forgets much of what he has read. The reason for reading all the books, and the meaning of life itself, falls through his fingers like sand. Just as a gross enjoyer loses pleasure for sense enjoyment as he grows older, the book collector becomes disappointed when he sees that all his reading has not improved him much as a person or brought him to even one simple conclusion. Near the end of his life, the actor Richard Burton, said that he wished to go to the grave crammed with knowledge. But what good is it to be packed with knowledge (or to be the possessor of thousands of books) if one goes to the grave and leaves behind all the knowledge in the library? The *Śrīmad-Bhāgavatam* declares that a person who owns many jewels and ornaments, including the ornament of education, but does not praise the Supreme Personality of Godhead, will sink down at the time of death—and his ornaments will be the cause of his drowning. One's library may do the same. The Japanese monk Gensei, predicted that because of his being a bookworm, he might become a silverfish (a little bug) who inhabits the pages of books.

A person interested in spiritual development also reads books, but he is warned of the danger of deviation through promiscuous book reading. Thus it is stated in *Śrīmad-Bhāgavatam,* "Literature that is a useless waste of time—in other words, literature without spiritual benefit—should be rejected" *(Bhāg.* 7.13.7). Śrīla Prabhupāda expands upon this in his purport:

> A person desiring to advance in spiritual understanding should be extremely careful to avoid reading ordinary literature. The world is full of

ordinary literature that creates unnecessary agitation in the mind. Such literature, including newspapers, dramas, novels and magazines, is factually not meant for advancement in spiritual knowledge. Indeed, it has been described as a place of enjoyment for crows *(tad-vāyasaṁ tīrtham)*. Anyone advancing in spiritual knowledge must reject such literature. Furthermore, one should not concern oneself with the conclusions of various logicians or philosophers. Of course, those who preach sometimes need to argue with the contentions of opponents, but as much as possible one should avoid an argumentative attitude.

—*Bhāg.* 7.13.7, purport

V

Malte Laurids Brigge
A Portrait of the Artist as a Young Neurotic

Under my father's direction, I joined the U.S. Naval Reserve in order to avoid being drafted into the army. For two weeks during one summer when I was in college, I had to go on a cruise. It was on a small ship like a destroyer escort. The cruise went somewhere north and visited a Canadian island. It only lasted two weeks, but I strongly disliked it. It was my first thrust into association with low sailors. They were career sailors, or at least they weren't reservists on a two-week cruise. There were only a few reservists, and we weren't even together on the ship. I hated waiting in the mess line and having to listen to the filthy language. I felt so alienated and unhappy to be there.

I remember a book that I had with me by the German poet Rilke. It was a fictional diary, The Notebooks of Malte Laurids Brigge. *The book is said to be a forerunner of other existential books like Sartre's fictional diary,* Nausea. *Just as the navy cruise was a jarring adventure for me, this book was also a trip. Rilke discussed the anguish of human existence in* any *situation. Life is absurd, every person is filled with dread when he considers his existence. Rilke portrayed a person who was sensitive to the point of being neurotic. He imagined things, and at the same time, actually felt things that other people did not.*

In a sense, you could say that reading this book worsened my condition, but in another sense, it provided shelter. There was somebody else who knew that life on the destroyer escort was not real life. Rilke was a shelter, but he was putting me into other kinds of internal knots.

I kept the book in my back pocket, not sticking out so they would see it like I did at the beach, but there. I didn't have any service on the ship. They assigned me to the radar room, but no one bothered to teach me anything. I just went in there and hung out. That was their attitude toward the two-week reserve man. They didn't harass me either. I sat there and would sometimes take out my book. On the cover it had an etching of Brigge. He had a black beard and black hair. I would pull it out of my navy dungaree pocket and read right there in the radar room. It didn't cause much interaction, although someone might briefly say, "What's that?" The waves tossed and churned. I didn't get sick, but it was like the nausea described by Sartre. Everything was part of the bad time.

The ship would lurch even on normal days, and I could feel it even down within the bowels of the ship where I slept. I had no work, and neither could I bear to talk with the guys, so I mostly stayed in my bunk. One friendly colored guy said, "What kinda job you got? You always sleepin' in the day, you must be a bartender." One day, while waiting on the chow line, I saw a poster of the obscure place in Canada where we were going to visit. One of the sailors pointed to the map saying, "See, you go over here and that's where the whorehouse is." I wasn't interested. I was in a different consciousness.

By the time I took the naval cruise, I had become sensitive to the point of preciosity. Bringing *Malte Laurids Brigge* as my companion and shelter only made me more aware that I was different and more refined than the rest. I got a double dose of misery. The cruise itself dished out one kind of misery, and existentialism served up another.

I remember a school teacher once commenting that "sensitive persons" are usually only sensitive about their own concerns, but they are not compassionate for the needs of others. When I heard it, I felt defensive, but I had to admit that it might be true. On board the navy ship, I felt consistently sorry for my own plight, but I didn't think much of the others who were also victims of various kinds of distress, even though they may not have expressed it like Ranier Maria Rilke.

A true transcendentalist would not have coiled in disgust when in the midst of animalistic men. Prahlāda Mahārāja did not reject the children of demons. He cheerfully tried to give them Kṛṣṇa consciousness. But I had nothing to share except *angst*, and even that was vague to me. I did not have much courage in my convictions, but was searching alone, drawn to the company of the alienated Malte Laurids Brigge.

My father saw the Navy as a means to improve my character, but I did not see it that way. Now I can understand that it did contribute to my well-being, but in a way neither my father nor I could have realized. The Navy was miserable. That in itself was a good preparation for seeking relief from all misery. *The Notebooks of Malte Laurids Brigge* threw away the veil of material happiness.

What was I getting from Rilke when I crammed *Malte* in a corner of the ship's radar room? I won't pretend that I understood it as a systematic philosophy, but I recall phrases, episodes, and the mood it evoked in me.

Malte was a poet living in Paris. He was a stranger among strangers. He was poor, and he lived among the poor. When he walked the streets he saw victims and visions of despair and death. One time he saw the remaining, interior wall of a demolished house. When he looked at it, it became a symbol of misery, shame, and decay. Malte ran away in horror from the wall, and he thought that everyone must be able to see that his soul had been exposed. It was depressing to read. Sometimes Malte seemed to see with a realistic eye, sometimes as a sensitive poet, and sometimes he seemed to be hallucinating. I couldn't relate to the scenes in which he saw ghosts. When he described himself being pursued by a nameless Fear or Thing, I worried about it. I hoped it wouldn't happen to me.

Rilke wrote, "Who speaks of victory? To endure is all." That struck a chord within me. Endure the

Navy; endure is all. In ways like that, he gave me strength to face the obscenities on the chow line.

God was frequently referred to in *Malte,* but Malte seemed to be a very complicated agnostic. He almost forgot God in the difficult work of approaching Him. The book ended with Malte talking about himself:

> How could they know who he was? He was now terribly difficult to love, and he felt that only One would be capable of it. But He was not yet willing.

God was unwilling to love him? Was this the symptom of a sensitive, deep poet? Should I be like that? Was it good or bad? Hmmm. I thought it over.

Malte had something strange to say about love. He seemed to say that he was yearning to love, but he could not stand being loved in return: "To be loved means to be consumed in flames. To love is to give light with an inexhaustible oil. To be loved is to pass away; to love is to endure."

It all haunted me. The intensity of it was like a fire to warm my cold spirit. Becoming an intellectual reader was hard work, and this was only one of innumerable books and authors—and each serious writer seemed to have his own private language and a separate view of existence. It was confusing. Even when I sometimes met a rare person with whom I could share such books, I found it hard to say much except, "I'm into it, I love it."

(118)

Did I really love *Malte Laurids Brigge,* or was it just a case of "misery loves company?" *I am glad I came to Kṛṣṇa consciousness!* Where would I be by now? Converted into an ordinary sailor rather than go on suffering in sensitivity? Gone the way of Malte and become an "existentialist?" Suicide by now? The alternatives were all unhappy *cul de sacs.*

VI

Paradise Lost

In my last year of college, I took a course taught by Professor Don Wolf, a specialist in the great British poet, John Milton. We studied Paradise Lost. *I was happy to possess a beautiful volume of the book and kept it in a plastic cover. Professor Wolf asked each student to memorize a sizable section from the epic and speak in front of the class. I chose a speech by Satan. I took pleasure in trying to give a relaxed, urbane version of the devil speaking.*

Milton was a religious thinker and his purpose in writing Paradise Lost *was to "justify the ways of God to man." But somehow, his humanlike portrait of Satan came off more successfully than God, Adam, or the angels and saintly persons. I also remember some of the students in our class protesting when Adam said that he wanted to have children in order to help in the gardening work in Paradise. The students thought this showed an exploitative motive of Adam as father. But Professor Wolf was always sympathetic to Milton and he tried to explain to us why Adam's desire for "extra hands" in the garden was not exploitative.*

I think the religious significance of the poem went over our heads. We were mostly concerned with trying to figure out the meanings so that we would be able to get good grades on the final exam. At the end of the semester, Professor Wolf again asked each of us to speak in front of the class and to tell personal things. I said, "After I graduate, I intend to go on and get a master's degree. And if worse comes to worst, I will get a PhD." That was my prepared comic line and it went over okay.

In 1966 when I read Prabhupāda's booklet, *Easy Journey to Other Planets,* I was pleased to note his reference to Milton. Prabhupāda writes, "The living of a miserable life in the material world by dint of the soul's choice, is nicely illustrated by Milton in *Paradise Lost.* Similarly, by choice, the soul can regain paradise and return home, back to Godhead." Unfortunately, we did not read the book for any spiritual significance. I read it because it was a classic and it was supposed to be cultural. Anyone who is a scholar in English literature must know it well. Occasionally, I received a glimpse of appreciation for the stately eloquence of Milton's blank verse:

> Of man's first disobedience and the fruit
> Of that forbidden tree, whose mortal taste
> Brought death into the world and all our woe,
> With loss of Eden, till one greater Man
> Restore us and regain the blissful seat,
> Sing heav'nly Muse, that on the secret top
> Of Oreb, or of Sinai, didst inspire
> That shepherd, who first taught the chosen seed,
> In the beginning how the heavens and earth
> Rose out of Chaos;

> . . . And chiefly thou, O Spirit, that doest prefer
> Before all temples th' upright heart and pure,
> Instruct me, for thou know'st; thou from the first
> Wast present, and with mighty wings outspread
> Dove-like sat'st brooding on the vast abyss,
> And mad'st it pregnant: what in me is dark
> O illumine, what is low raise and support;
> That to the height of this great argument
> I may assert eternal Providence,
> And justify the ways of God to men.

I found no religious inspiration while reading the great religious epic of English literature. Or if I did, I have completely forgotten it. The English department at Brooklyn College had no intention of preaching God consciousness. They saw such studies as sectarian religion. In fact, no department in any university is prepared to teach the *science* of God in a nonsectarian way. Prabhupāda personally delivered this challenge to the students of Massachusetts Institute of Technology when he lectured there—"Where is the department that teaches the science of the spirit soul?"—but it may also be delivered to every university in the world. And if one doesn't learn the science of the soul and the science of God, then his human life is wasted. So at the end of my fourth year of college, I had nothing to show in terms of self-realization, or knowledge of the science of God.

I suspected that Professor Wolf was religious himself, but he kept it carefully hidden. He loved Milton, but he taught him in an academic way as required by the syllabus. Milton himself was concerned with politics and sectarian religious beliefs.

Our book was filled with footnotes to explain Milton's attacks on contemporaries, especially the Papists, supporters of the Catholic Church. In the same way, Dante's *Inferno* is filled with footnotes to explain which enemies of the Church he was referring to when he placed them in different sections of hell. Except for these footnotes, everyone has forgotten the particulars of the religious-political squabbles from the days of Milton or Dante.

I wanted to be a sincere student of a great cultural work, even a religious work. Therefore, I enrolled in the course for *Paradise Lost*. But I lacked sincerity or any real drive to inquire about spiritual knowledge, and there was no one on the faculty of English literature who was teaching God consciousness. Milton's whole purpose was God consciousness, but it did not move us that way. We saw him as one of the big guns, the top greats in English literature, that's all. We were students or aspiring scholars, and so we knew we had to appreciate him.

My remark to the fellow students, "If worse comes to worst, I'll get a PhD," turned out to be something that never happened. The U.S. Navy stood in my way. I had to enter for two years of active service immediately after graduating with the Bachelor of Arts. I often think that if I had been allowed to pursue my studies for Master's and PhD degrees, I would have had less chance of becoming interested in Kṛṣṇa consciousness. So it seemed like the frustration of my desired career turned out to be the blessings of Providence.

4

On My Own

I

Entering a Cage of Fire

One morning in January, 1962, I said goodbye and left the house. I was dressed in navy blue, which is almost black. I was carrying a full navy dufflebag. I probably had a few books to read, which I must have chosen carefully, because you couldn't carry that many. It was a big bundle to carry on my shoulder. I could never walk continuously with it. I had to hoist it up onto my shoulder, and then stop and alternate shoulders as I walked. When I actually got somewhere, then I dragged it, a heavy, olive drab, canvas bag. I walked off with that bag, white sailor hat, peacoat, heavy bellbottom trousers and black shoes. It was early morning and a long way to the city. I was trying to summon whatever inner forces I had to sustain me.

The first place I reached in Lower Manhattan was just for signing papers. While waiting, I took a book out from the top of my bag. It was Short Stories of Ernest Hemingway. *Although he was renowned, I hadn't read him. Somebody asked me, "Hey, what's that?" I showed him and he said, "Oh, I've heard of him." I wanted to look at the craft of a recognized great writer like Hemingway. I was thinking as a writer because that's what I did: I was a writer. Hemingway stories.*

And he is a tough guy too. Tough stories. Maybe it was a good atmosphere for that.

Then we recruits were packed into a bus and taken to a military establishment in Brooklyn. It was painful. The barracks. Lots of double-decker beds, metal lockers, metal beds. Some guys there were on the tail-end of their service. Their attitude was, "Sure glad to get the f____ out of this place."

It is painful to have to talk to people you don't like or who you don't want to associate with. It is such a lonely thing. Although I have been saying that my reading into deep books and sensitive novels was just a pose, it wasn't a light pose. Over the years, I had actually developed into a sensitive poet, a fellow traveler with the writers of the great books I read. When I came in contact with uneducated, rough people, it was painful for me. They used foul speech and I recoiled from it. It hurt to be with them, but in the Navy, I had no choice. To constantly do what is painful, to live with those gross, horrible people—I couldn't be reached by my comrades, nor could I feel compassion for them. I was isolated. I felt like my spirit was being damaged, and my wings were clipped. Steppenwolfe, Look Homeward, Angel, *and what to speak of Rilke . . . they* cultured *the alienated and sensitive individual. Here I was, thrust into it.*

After recalling the painful time of joining the Navy, my first impulse is to assure myself that I am out of it. I am all right now. I live in the association of devotees. *I am grateful for Kṛṣṇa consciousness.*

When Lord Caitanya asked Rāmānanda Rāya what was the greatest unhappiness, Rāmānanda Rāya replied, "To be separated from the association of devotees." He said it was like being in a cage of fire.

What if I had to do it again, be in the Navy with foul-mouthed guys who don't like Kṛṣṇa? For one thing, I wouldn't allow myself to do it if it were at all possible to avoid. In my pre-Prabhupāda years I was so covered over, I didn't know that I could be who I actually was. I thought I had to do whatever my father and the government said. I did not know who I was, but even if I had known, I would not have dared to assert myself against the norm. It is not likely that I will have to go back into an imprisonment like that, but I still *dream* I am in the Navy. And when I wake from it, I think, "If you don't go back to Godhead, then next life, you may have to go through that again."

It still frightens me to recall those days. I am stronger now and willing to walk away from non-devotee situations. This is Prabhupāda's mercy. He has created temples and made people into devotees. I can go into a community of devotees and live with them. I don't have to be in a cage of fire. And if by some calamity I was suddenly forced to be among them, I would have something to live for, something I didn't have in 1962—Kṛṣṇa consciousness.

I don't know what is going to happen in my next life. Some *Bhāgavatam* passages I have read lately indicate to me the likelihood of returning again. You have to be perfect before you go to Goloka

Vṛndāvana for eternity, bliss, and knowledge. Prabhupāda writes:

> Actually, the pure devotee never thinks that he is fit for liberation. Considering his past life and his mischievous activities, he thinks that he is fit to be sent to the lowest region of hell. . . . A devotee always prays, "For my misdeeds, may I be born again and again, but my only prayer is that I may not forget Your service." The devotee has that much mental strength, and he prays to the Lord, "May I be born again and again, but let me be born in the home of Your pure devotee so that I may again get a chance to develop myself."
> —*Bhāg.* 3.25.40, purport

If this is the case, then I have to deepen my thinking of Kṛṣṇa. Then if I do come back, I can take up Kṛṣṇa consciousness and the association of the devotees of Śrīla Prabhupāda as soon as possible. We can often find prayers like this repeated by pure devotees—"My dear Lord, it does not matter where I am born, but let me be born even as an ant, in the house of a devotee. Please let me remember You." We may have to come back, so please Lord, give us strength to revive our lost consciousness. No more, "O lost, and by the wind grieved, ghost come back again." No more being completely crushed amid crude people. Please give me the consciousness of devotional service, life after life.

As for book-reading, please give me *Śrīmad-Bhāgavatam.* Hanging tough with Hemingway is not what I want. It didn't help *him* in the end. Give me young Śukadeva Gosvāmī. Give me the dust from the feet of the Vaiṣṇavas. I want these books. I want to *love* the *Śrīmad-Bhāgavatam,* but short of love, I cling to my identity as spirit soul. I am afraid of any other identity because I know it is empty—it contains no victory. Therefore, let me be a devotee of Kṛṣṇa, even though I may not have attained full depth, because all other options repel me.

Those sensitive authors who were my mentors, had a flickering of hope—that there is a better life. But the authors themselves could not or would not find it. When I carried them with me in my duffle bag into the hardest test of my life, they gave me their friendship, but they could not give me release. I forgive them, but I must not forget their shortcomings. Anyway, it is over now. My duty now is to not be an offender to the devotees, so that they will always allow me to serve in their company.

II

Decadence

Our ship went once a year to the Mediterranean and stopped in many ports. One time, as I walked past a bookstore in Cannes, France, I saw in the window editions of books that I had never seen in America. They were written in English and had green covers. They were printed by a French press that published English-speaking authors who had been censored in America. Some of the books were considered classics in literature, but they had been banned because of their obscene content. There were many volumes by Henry Miller, and there was also Jean Genet's A Thief's Journal. *It was exciting to see them. I bought two copies of* A Thief's Journal, *as well as Henry Miller's trilogy,* The Rosey Crucifixion, *and sent copies home to my friends in Brooklyn. They wrote back, thanking me: "We can't get these books here." This was the mood in the Mediterranean—cultural but decadent. So I became like the other sailors and went into bars where the girls were decadent. Or even if I went off by myself as I did in Capri, I was still under the influence of corruption. Sometimes I went into churches while drunk and my thoughts were self-centered and aesthetic. I got these attitudes from the decadent writers. Most sailors wouldn't read them because they were filled with intellectual meditations and speculations and they had the deep artistic intentions which are appreciated by scholars, writers, and artists. But they had the same amount of obscenity and graphic sexual descriptions that you find in trashy books. It seems fitting that when I was in the Navy, I should find these books and read them.*

I remember reading Henry Miller while on the ship, then finally getting disgusted. The sexual descriptions were too graphic. On the other hand, he had a dynamic approach to writing and literature. He wrote what he thought in a voice without artificiality or pretention.

Jean Genet was decadent in a different way. He would even use religious imagery to describe degraded things, like the life of a thief or homosexual, or of people dealing treacherously with one another. It shocked me, but I read it and took it in. He used religious literary expressions, aspirations for holiness, descriptions of saints, of God and worship, but he would use them to describe a fellow prisoner. He would write pages of an aesthetic essay on the striped uniforms that they wore in jail. Describing some tough, degraded cellmate, he would say something like, "When he sat down, it was like genuflecting before the altar." He used all kinds of sacred images to describe the most degraded things. He was not trying to create a cheap sensation, but he was trying to present a deep sense of what he was seeing in the most common, degraded things, a depth that most people see only in the exaltation of religion and transcendence. Although he wrote what people look for in sexually explicit books (and which publishers look for to increase sales), Genet's corruption was something even deeper.

The way he wrote about the lives of the perverts in Marseilles and Paris, or the crooks and people in jail, was really an intense experience because he was aesthetic and artistic.

He was a devilish figure. He himself was a thief, and for that and for many other crimes, he was in jail. He was supposed to be incarcerated for a long sentence, but all the famous French intellectuals sent a petition to the government, that this man was the greatest artist in France. They petitioned for his release so he could make his contribution to mankind. He had that kind of patronage although he was a thief and a pervert, not a scholar.

During this same period in the Navy, I also read Celine. He fit in perfectly. He was dynamite. I had to look a long time to find his books, Death on the Installment Plan *and* The Journey to the End of the Night. *My Brooklyn college friends, Steve Kowit, Murray Mednick and others, had a kind of cult of Celine appreciation at that time. One way to describe these authors is to take something I read in Henry Miller describing his own writing. In* Henry Miller on Writing, *the editors have taken out from his books just the aesthetic and intellectual parts that describe art. In the beginning of that book he writes, "Some people who are my avid readers, are attracted just to the obscene parts [of the literature]" (he probably did not use that word) "and some are attracted only to the intellectual parts and they don't read the obscene parts. But if you really want to understand me, it all goes together." Celine was the same kind of writer. One scholar said that Celine can be compared to filthy water. In this water, there are all kinds of horrible and dirty things, and there is also gold and other valuable ingredients, but there is no way to separate them. It all just comes out like that, wonderful bilge. Celine had a cynical, misanthropic attitude. He hated humanity and he told it like-it-is—that people are dogs, people are cruel, they torture each other in wars, they are pigs when they engage in sex life. It was like he was saying, "I do it too, let's face it, this is what humanity is. It is the scumming dregs, and any pretention to something higher is hypocritical." He wrote one book all about World War I, describing the cruelty of man to man, including details of murder, torture, and rape. And then he wrote another book about his growing up. My college friends and I saw him as a real writer. It seemed like the fitting time to read him, when my life was forced into corruption. I remember a Staten Island friend of mine telling me that the Navy would be like a candy bar for me. He said that I was a sensitive person, but I would not be able to refrain from eating the candy bar of the Navy, which would corrupt me with coarseness. In a sense he was right: I had to indulge in decadence, but I did it mostly through literature. I thought I was reading great literature, being unpretentious.*

During the period of my life in which I became physically and culturally decadent, there was no one who could convince me to uplift myself. I had parents, military authorities, religious chaplains, and many other moralists, but even if some of them occasionally said, "Save yourself!" it fell on deaf ears. How could I save myself? As far as I could see, there was nothing better. The morals of the Church's teachings never grasped my life with any depth. Why should I listen to parents or military? They never really cared for me or honored who I was. They did not know what I was going through. And they themselves were corrupt. My highest model for life was literature and art. But this is where art and reading seemed to lead, to an ultimate kind of aesthetic decadence. At the time, this seemed to me more true than the mere academic look into life as taught by Professor Solomon and his colleagues. Now I had found earthy artists, Henry Miller and company. They seemed to be more true, and I could not deny it. How could I save myself when I did not even know that there was any self to save, except for the self of the body, the mortal life?

I think differently now. I want to keep corruption far away. The world is corrupt and people are corrupt, but we don't have to become like that. We can protect ourselves. Kṛṣṇa consciousness gives us the strength. Nowadays, I am more attracted to actual saints and not to those author-heroes of my Navy days. The saintly person can live in the world, and even mix with the criminals and perverts, without becoming corrupt. Why does he mix with them? To help them. A devotee of God faces the reality and experience of life by serving God and helping others. He ministers to the needs of people, especially their spiritual needs. Preachers who take this risk are praised in the scriptures as more compassionate than solitary meditators and *yogīs.* Śrīla Prabhupāda writes, "One who is not very expert in preaching may chant in a secluded place, avoiding bad association, but for one who is actually advanced, preaching and meeting people who are not engaged in devotional service are not disadvantages. A devotee gives the nondevotees his association but is not affected by their misbehavior. Thus by the activities of a pure devotee, even those who are bereft of love of Godhead get a chance to become devotees of the Lord one day" (*Cc. Ādi* 7.92, purport). Śrīla Prabhupāda did this himself, approaching "the world's toughest audience, junkies, acid-heads, pot-heads, etc.," in New York City.

But there is a limit to mixing with nondevotees in the corrupt world. A devotee does not adopt the behavior of criminals. He does not degrade himself or give up his regular spiritual practices of cleanliness, celibacy, chanting and hearing the holy names and pastimes of Kṛṣṇa. He lives with likeminded pure devotees, and goes with them to preach in the cities. This is the way to face the fact that we live in a corrupt world. Save yourself from it first, and then try to save others. Do not become one of the fallen in the name of being "real" or "gaining experience." If you do that, you will be lost in the process. (I remember Śrīla Prabhupāda trying to convince a Christian priest that we should avoid killing animals at all costs. The priest replied, "Well, it is a fallen world." Prabhupāda responded, "Yes, but you don't have to be fallen also.")

(130)

I was reading books that were not recommended to me by the "elders" of society and government, and there was pleasure in that. I was searching for honesty, and I appreciated it in these authors. But their *mixture* of corruption and art was degrading. As I see it now, they did not give a clear spiritual message. As we cannot dismiss the honesty of these authors, neither can we dismiss the need for literatures that will save us at the time of death. It is not a small omission when writers do not know anything about the self. If a dog could write, it would also give us an honest account, which might produce a thrilling kind of literature never before experienced. But by reading the dog's life, a man could not solve his greatest problems. Literature should be more than mere entertainment or even thoughtfulness or "honesty," which are all very limited. We should be able to have all the entertainment value and honesty that any ordinary man or dog—or extraordinary author—can provide, but at the same time, we should be able to hear from someone who is trying to free himself from birth and death, and who is following reliable authorities. Whatever "dynamite" charge is in those authors, it comes from the Supersoul within each person's heart. The same honesty to experience and unpretention, can also be used in Kṛṣṇa's service. New vistas of Kṛṣṇa conscious literature can be written by honest persons confronting life, but uplifting us instead of pushing our faces in the muck.

We can hardly trust with all our hearts, the authors I mentioned, who all delve in the sensational.

The dictionary defines sensationalism as "the use of strongly emotional subject matter, or wildly dramatic style, language or artistic expression, that is intended to shock, startle, thrill, excite, etc." Preoccupation with or exploitation of the sensational in literature and art, is no longer honesty or humanness. Even honesty by itself is not enough, especially if one is candid but happens to have an uneducated or twisted vision of life. In that case, one's art power can mislead others. Sometimes authors gain a big following of readers by their *śakti* and honest expression and startling literary turns. But eventually, the writer admits to his followers that he is actually a cheater, and that both he and they have wasted their lives.

These books were censored in the early 1960s and now they are not. Now they may be considered great art, but in later years, they may again fall into ill repute and be considered tawdry. Kṛṣṇa conscious literature is not subject to such change. It is always good and fresh. There is no suspicion that it may degrade us, or that the author may be a hoax, or that in the future, his good standing will diminish like a failure on the stock exchange.

When we hear that in Vedic culture there was some form of censorship, it is sometimes difficult to fit that in with our modern liberal thinking. I am not prepared to discuss the sensitive and complex subject of government control and individual rights—but I may at least mention here that an individual should apply his own kind of censorship or discrimination in reading. One should not just go for that which is sensational or the lastest trend. We should be able to tell if we are getting nourishment from the books we are reading. One should take what is good for him, as we do in food, and not eat junk "foods" which are harmful.

What I write here may seem too moralistic for some. I do not dismiss these writers simply as bad men. But I do not want to approve them. My search for honesty took me there, but I had hardly found the ultimate shelter in the hands of Miller, Genet, and Celine.

III

Kierkegaard and Rilke: Friends in the Difficult

Even when crossing the Atlantic ocean, I had some books with me. I thought of my favorite great authors as intimate friends. My sister used to chide me, "You think that you are some kind of soul-brother with great poets and writers?" She meant that I was being pretentious, and that I had no right to think of myself as almost equal with great writers. But she did not understand that I was *intimate with those authors, and we were fellow sufferers.*

One of the authors I remember reading on the U.S.S. Saratoga was Soren Kierkegaard. How did he come to me? Maybe I had picked up one of his books when browsing in the Eighth Street bookstore. His volumes used to be more prominently displayed than most philosophers. Besides that, his titles appealed to me, An Attack on Christendom, The Sickness Unto Death, *and* Fear and Trembling. *The portrait of his face was also interesting, with a large 19th Century collar and a big shock of hair. I had put him somewhere in my duffle bag. Also in my bag was a book of letters to a poet, written by Ranier Maria Rilke. A young man had written to Rilke asking how he could know if he had a vocation as a writer. Rilke replied that in the very quiet moment, as deeply as possible, you should ask yourself, "Is it possible that I might* not *be a writer? If you honestly answer to yourself that it is not possible to be anything but a writer, then you have a vocation." These themes seemed extremely relevant to my case, and I kept them close to me.*

I have a visual memory of walking the deck of the U.S.S. Saratoga at night while she was in port, and thinking thoughts from Soren Kierkegaard. The reality of the ship became a mere background while I became absorbed in philosophy and grew sick in spirit. Was Kierkegaard's spirit sick? Was I sick? Or was sickness and despair the human condition? One of his chapters was titled, "The Universality of This Sickness, Despair." Even the mention of the words and concepts of Soren Kierkegaard was enough to drive me inward and melancholy. Despair. Sin. Guilt. Dread. Anxiety. Absurd.

Since that time, I have read more of Kierkegaard, and I now understand that in the Navy, I was reading his "indirect" books. In his later writings, he came out more directly as a Christian philosopher. In any case, it is not my purpose now, and neither do I have the ability, to describe his systematic thought.*

---

* I have not attempted to explain what I meant by my experience of a sickness of spirit, and neither have I done much explicating of the writings of Kierkegaard and Rilke.

Images from his books struck me. He said that the difference between theory and realization in spiritual matters is like the difference between reading a cookbook and actually cooking. But if Kierkegaard's grappling was "the real thing," it did not make me satisfied or happy. He gave me thought-substance. His was an urging toward self-realization. He said that no one could know the truth on one's behalf, one has to understand it oneself. Although he was always subtle and complex, he wrote with concrete, dramatic and personal expression. He sarcastically chastised the superficial life and those who have no inner reality. He was also against intellectual speculators. He demanded commitment. He pushed me to inner life. But from reading him, I could neither understand nor see the

---

In order to actually give comparative literary or philosophical analyses of these thinkers, I would have to study them again. That is not my intention in this book, but mostly to share the impressions that I retain of the days when I was reading my way through life, before meeting Śrīla Prabhupāda. A rigorous analysis of the actual thought of these authors might also prove a valuable study for a Kṛṣṇa conscious person. But Śrīla Prabhupāda tells us that it is not really necessary. Since such a rigorous study is not my intention, I hope that my focus on recalling my impressions will find sympathy with some readers. I know my situation is not that unusual, and that many persons in my generation read the same books and went through the same changes. By going back once again, and recalling the outlines of what we went through, I hope we may achieve a further purification. We have to conclude once and for all that we do not need books of mental speculation, and that the world of art—if it is without Kṛṣṇa—is another *cul de sac.* And I hope reviewing the memories of our search will increase our gratitude for what we have been given by Śrīla Prabhupāda in the Gauḍīya-Vaiṣṇava *sampradāya.*

light. I sensed that I was coming to grips with a spiritual sickness, and that he was an influence.

The Rilke book in my duffle bag was *Letters to a Young Poet.* The letters were actual correspondence between the great German poet and a young man who was aspiring to be a writer. At one point in the letters, the young man writes Rilke that he has now been inducted into the army. The boy is very downhearted about this and asks for advice. Rilke writes back that the suffering he will have to undergo in the army is a great opportunity for him. It will teach him "the difficult." Rilke went on to expound that "the difficult" is actually the deepest meaning in life, and if one wants to be a poet, then he should face it and learn it.

> And you should not let yourself be confused in your solitude by the fact that there is something in you that wants to break out of it. This very wish will help you, if you use it quietly, and deliberately and like a tool, to spread out your solitude over wide country. People have (with the help of conventions) oriented all their solutions toward the easy and toward the easiest side of the easy; but it is clear that we must hold to what is difficult; everything alive holds to it, everything in Nature grows and defends itself in its own way and is characteristically and spontaneously itself, seeks at all costs to be so and against all opposition. We know little, but that we must hold to what is difficult is a certainty that will not forsake us; it is good to be solitary, for solitude is difficult; that something is difficult must be a reason the more for us to do it.

How should it not be difficult for us?

And to speak of solitude again, it becomes always clearer that this is at bottom not something that one can take or leave. We *are* solitary. We may delude ourselves and act as though this were not so. That is all. But how much better it is to realize that we are so, yes even to begin by assuming it.

So you must not be frightened, dear Mr. Kappus, if a sadness rises up before you larger than any you have ever seen; if a restiveness, like light and cloud-shadows, passes over your hands and over all you do. You must think that something is happening with you, that life has not forgotten you, that it holds you in its hand; it will not let you fall. Why do you want to shut out of your life any agitation, any pain, any melancholy, since you really do not know what these states are working upon you? Why do you want to persecute yourself with the question whence all this may be coming and whither it is bound? Since you know that you are in the midst of transitions and wished for nothing so much as to change. If there is anything morbid in your processes, just remember that sickness is the means by which an organism frees itself of foreign matter; so one must just help it to be sick, to have its whole sickness and break out with it, for that is it progress. In you, dear Mr. Kappus, so much is now happening; you must be patient as a sick man and confident as a convalescent; for perhaps you are both. And more: you are the doctor too, who has to watch over himself. But there are in every illness many days when the doctor can do nothing but wait. And this it is what you, insofar as you are your own doctor, must now above all do.

Kierkegaard and Rilke impressed upon me that the human condition is very unhappy. I also felt unhappy, at least while in the Navy, and so their friendship was a solace to me.

I was too sensitive to be happy in the prison of the Navy, although they supplied material needs. I needed to live and breathe in a rarer atmosphere. Like everyone else, I wanted sense gratification, but I also needed more than I could find by life on the ship (or in the pleasure ports), and if I did not find it, I thought that I might die of suffocation. So I turned to books. In his fable, "The Hunger Artist," Franz Kafka tells of a professional starvation artist who is in a circus. He performs great feats of fasting, but no one knows the inner reason why he does it. Finally, when he is about to die of fasting, the hunger artist is asked why he does not eat. He replies, "Because I can never find anything suitable to eat." I took this to be a portrait of any artist. Ordinary people cannot understand. He dies in their midst, seeking something heavenly, unable to eat the crude food of life.

Whereas previously I may have been largely posing in the role of a sensitive soul, I now felt that I was struggling for survival in a real sense. I *was* actually alienated in the Navy, and I desperately sought assurance that my alienation was worthy, was something sacred. In order to deal with my situation, I usually played a deadpan role as an ordinary citizen of the ship, but my mind had learned to rise above the surroundings, like a water mammal coming up for air.

Unfortunately, I was not much concerned with survival after death. I was not thinking, "Is there life after death? Can the soul survive?" My concern was, how can I live now in this Navy? Can my spirit keep alive today despite all this crap? I rose above it by reading books that had spiritual content, although they were confusing, and I also thought to the future when I would be discharged from the Navy and move to the Lower East Side of New York to do what I wanted. Through books and thoughts I proved to myself that the mind can transcend the local place and be aware of a better clime. Even when my mind could not make the leap, my intelligence came forward with the steadying advice, "I am not a sailor actually; I will get out in less than two years."

During this time my thought was not religious. I did not consider that there was anything higher than the mind and intelligence. Neither did the authors whom I read inform me about factual spirituality. I did not know how the soul may know itself and how he may commune with the Supreme. Therefore, whatever "rising above" I managed, it was not transcendental. I could not go beyond human experience; I was not aware of God. I was heading in that direction, but still working on the preliminary methods for daily survival. By pondering philosophical dilemmas of human spirit in material existence, as described in Kierkegaard and Rilke, I was able to escape the pain and deadening life of the Navy.

What I had learned was a kind of flight with the wings of the mind. I did it because my own mind was so dissatisfied and I knew *there was more to life than this.* Śrīla Prabhupāda speaks of this yearning to be free which occurs to the imprisoned self. But for Śrīla Prabhupāda and the Vedic sages, real freedom occurs when the absolute self reaches the absolute abode of freedom:

> The body and the mind are but superfluous outer coverings of the spirit soul. The spirit soul's needs must be fulfilled. Simply by cleansing the cage of the bird, one does not satisfy the bird. One must actually know the needs of the bird himself.
>
> The need of the spirit soul is that he wants to get out of the limited sphere of material bondage and fulfill his desire for complete freedom. He wants to get out of the covered walls of the greater universe. He wants to see the free light and the spirit. That complete freedom is achieved when he meets the complete Spirit, the Personality of Godhead.
>
> —*Bhāg.* 1.2.8, purport

Instead of finding salvation or transference to the fountainhead of all liberties, I was reading books that made me think that existence was innately unhappy, and that I should learn to endure it. On the one hand, my author-friends helped me to endure "the difficult," and yet they left me in a strange and unhappy consciousness. I was not even sure of *what* they were saying; it certainly was not a message of peace and joy.

As I recall the books in my life, especially during this critical period, I can understand the danger of the eclectic type of reading I was doing. One becomes enamoured with one writer after another, and all the different views begin to bounce around inside. You remain uncommitted, but you become addicted to the habit of tasting deep thoughts with no final conclusion. I was particularly impressionable. To escape the Navy, I sometimes indulged in hedonism and depravity through Henry Miller and Jean Genet. Then during the same day, I would turn to the ascetic Soren Kierkegaard, who was celibate and cerebral-spiritual. With an attitude like mine, even if I had chanced upon some Vedic texts, I would have probably treated them in the same way. Besides, without the guidance of a spiritual master, even Vedic scriptures can remain impenetrable.

Now I think differently. There *is* a spiritual world and a practical process to reach it, *bhakti-yoga.*

> This knowledge is the king of education, the most secret of all secrets. It is the purest knowledge, and because it gives direct perception of the self by realization, it is the perfection of religion. It is everlasting, and it is joyfully performed
>
> —*Bg.* 9.2.

The human dilemma is not as bad as the existentialists portray. There will always be misery as long as we remain in the material world, but beyond the cycle of birth and death, there is another nature, and it is eternal (*Bg.* 8.20). What in former ages was always "the difficult," even for profound philosophers and ascetics, has now been made accessible and even easy. This is because the supreme truth, in the form of Lord Caitanya, has made spiritual perfection attainable for everyone. I now see the atheistic or religious existentialists that I used to read as great mental speculators, and I see some of them as tremendously sincere souls seeking the way out of the material maze, unable to find the goal. I no longer read them, because I have to save myself from death.

IV

A Zen Friend

One day on the chow line, I saw a man in front of me with a copy of Zen Flesh, Zen Bones, *by Paul Reps, peeking out of the back pocket of his denims. Just to see that book, which I had already read, created a little moment of* satori. *It was a yellow paperback with a woodblock illustration on the cover of a Japanese boy with a pigtail, playing on a flute and riding a bull. So I spoke to the sailor carrying* Zen Flesh. *His name was Henry. He was tall and gentle with an enigmatic little smile. Something about him reminded me of a comic strip character called "Henry," who was bald and who wore short pants and who did mysterious, funny things. The Navy Henry looked innocent and cherubic. When I mentioned that I had read* Zen Flesh, *we struck up an immediate friendship. He seemed not so much interested in Chinese or Japanese history or philosophy, as in seeing Zen in the everyday.*

I recall Henry sitting in a half-lotus position on an office chair. We met on different occasions and shared insights that helped to uplift us from the Navy ordeal. I remember a valuable insight he gave me for tolerating our foul-mouthed shipmates. "I see them as furry," he said. He meant, don't hate them. Just as you don't hate a furry wild animal just because it is less educated and refined than yourself, so you should have compassion even for the lowlife sailors. I liked that and it helped.

One time after walking on the flight deck, I had come down to the office shivering. I happened to meet Henry there and mentioned to him how cold it was topside. He said, "Sometimes it's good to become chilled." I suppose this was an ordinary remark, but somehow things were not ordinary between us. We sensed a special life going on, because we knew the Zen potentials of waking up in every ordinary moment.

I could not tell Henry about my secret weapon for transforming consciousness, my private joint smoking on the admiral's catwalk. But we shared what we could. I think we lacked a more old-fashioned honesty in our talks. We did not unwind and tell each other of our backgrounds, our hopes and desires. We did not think that such behavior was Zen-like. Yet my meetings with him were a bright light. We both knew that we were imprisoned, but we attempted to help each other by odd and oblique insights into reality.

I suspected that maybe Zen could be used as a façade, a way to avoid looking directly at the hurt inside. Perhaps Henry thought there was no point in looking inside in an emotional way. So mostly we played a game, thinking of clever "Zen" ways to see the oppressive reality of imprisonment upon the "Suckin' Saratoga."

As for *Zen Flesh, Zen Bones,* it contained stories like this one:

> Tanzan and Ekido were once traveling down a muddy road together. A heavy rain was still falling. Coming around a bend they saw a lovely girl in a silk kimono and sash unable to cross the intersection.
>
> "Come on, girl," Tanzan said at once. Lifting her in his arms, he carried her over the mud.
>
> Ekido did not speak again until that night when they reached a lodging temple. Then he no longer could contain himself. "We monks don't go near females," he told Tanzan, "especially not young and lovely ones. It is dangerous. Why did you do that?"
>
> "I left the girl there," said Tanzan. "Are you still carrying her?"

The most far-out thing about the book was the way it ended. The next to last page was titled, "What is Zen?" It gave a few explanations, but at the very bottom of the page it said, "Another answer:"—and when you turned the page, you were faced with a blank. So that is the answer, Nothingness. Later when we were both out of the navy, Henry and I met again, but later, we lost contact. I still think of him sometimes, and wonder whether he might have become interested in Kṛṣṇa consciousness. I wonder what became of him, and whether he is still looking at the blank page:

You cannot describe it, you cannot picture it,
you cannot admire it, you cannot sense it.
It is your true self, it has nowhere to hide.
When the world is destroyed it will be destroyed.

—*Zen Flesh, Zen Bones*

V

Franz Kafka's Diaries

I received an honorable discharge from the Navy in January of 1964. My new freedom was euphoric, but gradually it turned to tears of hurt and LSD madness. For a couple of years, I moved from apartment to apartment in Manhattan, including Suffolk Street, Second Street, an apartment near the George Washington Bridge, Eleventh Street—and when I ran out of money and health, I moved back to Staten Island and my parents' home. I took a part-time job in the city, but it didn't make much sense. It took me almost two hours traveling each way, just for a few dollars. But I couldn't just "hang around" (as my parents saw it). It was during this time that I started reading Franz Kafka's diaries, which I had purchased in two hardbound volumes from the Eighth Street bookstore.

I read his diaries with more intensity than I read his novels, which sometimes became tedious. Now I saw him not only as Kafka the Great Novelist, but as a companion.

Kafka was constantly facing what Rilke called "the difficult." He faced it with inflexible intellectual honesty and sensitivity.

The diary was satisfactory reading, even though it was not intended for readers. My mind could go over the unconnected passages and quickly understand all that it needed to, even more than in the fictional story. It was like looking through a peephole—to see a disturbed young genius in his little room within the apartment of his parents in Prague, Czechoslovakia.

From his photo, Kafka was a good-looking man, but his face was mysterious, like a cat's face. It was the face of he who wrote The Castle, The Trial, *and who wrote in his diary, "But I must not forsake myself." He described himself as a weak and faithless soul. I saw him as a saint turned inside out. From his picture, he also looked like an official working in an insurance company. He saw deeply into his own existence, and yet could not accept the grace of God. He thought that grace was not possible.** *He predicted, twenty years in advance, the Holocaust, in his story, "The Penal Colony." His face was in my book on the shelf; he traveled with me on the Staten Island ferry and we came home together each night.*

---

* Kafka seems to have assumed from the beginning that there was no Supreme Being. At least he could not find Him, could not see Him anywhere in a wretched material world. So he concluded that all hope of God was in vain—and God was a myth, as problematic as a bureaucratic state trial, or a castle that never lets you know its intentions. He had no guru, no *paramparā*, for he was not born at the right time. But he will come again and will get credit for his honesty. Śrīla Prabhupāda said of similar authors that their sincerity is their God consciousness.

His diary was not something to play around with, but I felt that I was serious enough to read it properly. He made me aware that I too was confused and lost, and he was helping me. He was extremely scrupulous and humble. I remember one time telling my friend Murray, "Kafka said that people should not associate with him because he was not good for them." Murray and I both loved Kafka's truthfulness. Here is an excerpt from his diary:

> Today, for instance, I acted three pieces of insolence toward the conductor, toward someone introduced to me—well, there were only two but they hurt like a stomach ache. On the part of anyone, they would have been insolent, how much more so on my part.

Yes, he especially should not be insolent. He was piercingly honest about his own weakness and duplicity. You could not help but think, "Is that me also?"

> Together with Blie, his wife and child. From time to time, I listened to myself outside of myself, it sounded like the whimpering of a young cat.

> . . . The burning electric light, the silent house, the darkness outside, the last waking moments that give me the right to write, even if it be only the most miserable stuff. And this right I used hurriedly. That's the person I am.

> 28 December. When I have acted like a human being for a few hours, as I did today with Max

> and later at Baum's, I am already full of conceit before I go to sleep.

Sometimes Franz Kafka made you want to cry out, "Enough."

> Sunday, 19 July, slept, awoke, slept, awoke, miserable life.
>
> 25 November. Utter despair. Impossible to pull myself together; only when I have become satisfied with my sufferings can I stop.

Some of it rubbed off on you and you started seeing through his eyes. I was good at that too, falling into imitation.

> I have continually an invocation in my ear: "For you to come, invincible judgement!" It's 11:30 P.M. So long as I'm not freed of my office, I am simply lost, that is clearer to me than anything else, it is just a matter, as long as it is possible, of holding my head so high that I do not drown.

Kafka often expressed his impossible dilemma: He used most of his time and energy at his job in the office and did not have enough time to write. He also had a huge problem with his father, and wrote him a long letter which I don't think his father ever saw. In one entry, he tells how when he was younger, he was writing a story at the dinner table and an uncle picked it up, read it and said, "The usual stuff." He usually was not able to write. He sometimes felt "the imminent possibility of great moments which would tear me open, which would make me capable of anything." But then those inspirations faded away.

They will ask, "Are you praising Franz Kafka?" I say, "Be sorry for him, commiserate with him. Don't attack him." A disciple once said to Prabhupāda (concerning some atheists), "We will defeat them!" "Not defeat," said Śrīla Prabhupāda, "they are already defeated. Give them mercy."

I have written about Franz Kafka harshly in my *Journal & Poems*, although I acknowledged a debt. How does one acknowledge the debts from one's youth to authors you can no longer be true to? You do not want to say of either Kafka or Kierkegaard, "He screwed me up." You were already screwed up. And do not say, "He gave me a bad philosophy and a bad example to support my being screwed up."

They are different cases than you are, and each will be judged by his own merit only. They were not *trying* to mislead. At death, Kafka asked Max Brod to burn all the manuscripts, but Brod decided to save them.

Then what do you want to do, *pray* for them? Yes, a devotee should pray for everyone, why not them? If I consider my mother and father to be victims and not wrongdoers, and yet they were shallow people, why should I castigate my old authors? I will tell you why: because they were proud. Śrīla Prabhupāda used to call the demon a demon, a *mūḍhā* a *mūḍhā*.

"Do you mean to say that such a respectable person, such a great author or humanitarian is a *mūḍhā* and rascal just because he doesn't worship Kṛṣṇa?" Yes, yes, and it is not my manufacture. Kṛṣṇa says so in *Bhagavad-gītā, avajānanti māṁ mūḍhā.*

I abide with that judgement on the *muḍhās.* Still, I admire. I too am a *mūḍhā,* but at least I do not defy God. I am blessed. More reason then, to be kind to all, including old authors. It does not mean that you let their doubts contaminate you. Do not recommend them to others. Just settle your old account. Be kind to all. Say farewell—but even their famous names must be left behind.

They did not know better. They were not "lucky." Now save yourself and do not spread the infamy of their lack of faith in God. Come out of the darkness into the light.

And there is no time to lose; I need to read *Śrīmad-Bhāgavatam* steadfastly, daily, always. If you remember their names at all, Franz Kafka, etc., let it be in order to say a prayer for their restless souls. Only God can deliver them now.

VI

Tao Te Ching: A Preface to God

I got a job with the welfare department of New York City, and moved from my parents' house to my own apartment on the north shore of Staten Island. One day in that St. George apartment, with plain off-white walls, I sat on the bed and tried to do Nothing. I just sat there and thought, "Is this the Tao?" But my whole life at that time was meaningless. I felt it then, *especially when a young boy told me, "You've got nothing!" I recall waking one morning and visualizing the insides of the refrigerator where there were only a few slices of cold meat. It seemed like a symbol of my sterility—cold meat, no friends, and little hope. So when I read Lao Tse and some of Chuang Tzu, I somehow extracted out of it—wrongly or rightly—a hunch that I should just sit down on my bed and do nothing. But it soon became dry and purposeless. I gave it up after an hour or so, but thought, "Maybe you have to practice it a long time, or else you don't have the right idea at all."*

The ancient Taoists were mystics. Was I one? What did it mean to me? As I try to recall, I think of what Western philosophers signify when they say "speculation." They use the word favorably, as metaphysical insight. In my paperback approach to "The Way," I was speculating. I ruminated while riding on the Staten Island ferry. The call from the East to Something Beyond appealed to me. I liked the peace of "The Way" and the gentle word play. My quick loyalties were aroused, and so it became "a thing" for me. In Taoism I found "a new bag."

> It blunts sharpness,
> Resolves tangles;
> It tempers light,
> Subdues turmoil.
>
> A deep pool it is,
> Never to run dry!
> Whose offspring it may be
> I do not know:
> It is like a preface to God.
> —(4)

I could not exactly apply any of this in my welfare office. Yet it was not something that you had to act on. My reading of "The Way" gave me a new confidence that there was *something* other than what was happening externally. The poems of Lao Tse seemed to say it was okay if you do not know what it is, as long as you know that *it is.*

> I do not know its name;
> A name for it is "Way."
> Pressed for a designation,
> I call it Great.
> Great means outgoing,

Outgoing, far-reaching,
Far-reaching, return.
—(25)

The Way taught the philosophy of "let it be." But working in the city, I could not do much of that: "By letting go, it all gets done; the world is won by those who let it go!" (48) Neither did I have friends or sages to share it with deeply. But that was all right—it was something to hold inside. At least part of me aspired to be quiet, no matter what was going on; The Way was unfolding.

Touch ultimate emptiness,
Hold steady and still.

. . . This, I say, is the stillness,
A retreat to one's roots;
Or better yet, return
To the will of God . . .
—(16)

What shall I say now about The Way? I do not want to reject it all as "nonsense Chinese voidism." Personally, it gave me gentle hope that there was a Center to all existence. It was literally a preface to God, a getting ready for the Wiseman who would soon appear in my life. I know Godbrothers who also think fondly of their pre-Kṛṣṇa conscious reading of Lao Tse. As long as we accepted the teachings of *Bhagavad-gītā* when they came to us from Śrīla Prabhupāda, we were not harmed, but benefited by genuine mystical teachings. Even the *Vedas* are arranged in progression:

> When the activities for sense gratification, namely the *karma-kāṇḍa* chapter, are finished, then the chance for spiritual realization is offered in the form of the *Upāniṣads*, which are part of different *Vedas*, as the *Bhagavad-gītā* is part of the fifth *Veda*, namely the *Mahābharata*. The *Upāniṣads* mark the beginning of transcendental life. . . . This transcendental position is achieved in full Kṛṣṇa consciousness when one is fully dependent on the good will of Kṛṣṇa.
>
> —*Bg.* 2.45, purport

Lao Tse did not negate God consciousness for me. He was only reticent. The same is true of Confucius: "Tze Kung said, Our Master's views on culture and refinement are for all to hear, but what he has to say about the nature of man and the ways of God, no one ever hears" (Analects, V:XII).

In the Mentor edition of *Tao Te Ching* which I read, there is also this statement about Confucius: "The great Chinese felt that he had been divinely appointed to teach moral excellence and he would not say more than he knew. 'God begot the virtue in me. It was not my own'" (p. 17).

In a life puncuated with LSD hallucinations and heartbreak and dryness, the Old Ones' poems were moral and uplifting. And this was at a time when I thought I was too hip to take moral advice from the usual sources. Lao Tse was one of those first instructors who introduce you to the path. He did not hurt me with his "preface to God," and even now I see it with a "swanning" eye. By Prabhupāda's grace, I can draw the milk out of the mixture of water and milk. Yes, The Way cannot be named. He is *adhokṣaja*. He deliberately resists your attempts to know Him.

> Deluded by the three modes (goodness, passion, and ignorance) the whole world does not know Me who am above the modes and inexhaustible.
>
> —*Bg.* 7.13

> I am never manifest to the foolish and unintelligent. For them I am covered by My internal potency, and therefore they do not know that I am unborn and infallible.
>
> —*Bg.* 7.25

With our blunt senses we cannot see Kṛṣṇa; we cannot chant the name of God. But, by the mercy of Lord Caitanya, the most magnanimous of all Wisemen, we can begin to purify our minds and senses and chant the holy names. Then we may behold the inconceivable form of the Supreme Lord. So The Way which was revealed by mystics throughout the centuries in many lands is one way, seen variously according to the viewpoints of the different teachers, and distinguished by factors of time, persons, and place. The highest feature of The Way is *bhakti-yoga,* love of Kṛṣṇa.

> This, I say, is the stillness:
> A retreat to one's roots;
> Or better yet, return
> To the will of God.
>
> —(16)

VII

Reading Scriptures

While on an LSD trip, I began reading the Mentor edition of the Upāniṣads *and became totally bewildered. I could not distinguish between the material circumstances of my room, and the transcendental realm described by the book. One thing led to another and somehow or other, I fell out of the window and broke both my heels in a four-story fall. I spent the next six weeks in leg casts in my parents' home. Since I could not walk, I read a lot.*

I asked my mother for her Bible. I started reading systematically from the beginning, all the books of the Old Testament. It was very hard to understand, Book of this, Book of that, and I did not have any commentaries. But I continued faithfully reading the Old and New Testaments. My mother was pleased to see me reading, like the time when I was a kid and sang the Christmas carols that she had liked.

I also mailed away for a bunch of Eastern books from Mentor Paperbacks. I had the Upāniṣads *and the* Tao Te Ching, *and now I got* Bhagavad-gītā, Teachings of the Compassionate Buddha, The Teachings of Confucius. *My mother was suspicious of the East.*

"You don't really believe in that, do you?" she asked.

"No, I don't really believe it. But I am interested in it."

I remember thinking that I liked the Upāniṣads *better than the* Bhagavad-gītā. *Kṛṣṇa was asking Arjuna to fight, and that threw me off. Why should He ask him to fight? But there were parts of the* Bhagavad-gītā *that appealed to me, and I read them again and again. "All beings are born from the manifest, they live for awhile, and then they again become unmanifest when they are annihilated. So what need is there for lamentation?" It was a transcendental mystery. I was thinking, let me read all these pure spiritual teachings instead of other literature. These wise persons who lived over the centuries, Kṛṣṇa, the Buddha, Lao Tse, Jesus Christ, Moses, Confucius—I was revelling in the spiritual teachers. Partly I did it in order to get rid of the fear of the Evil that had manifested to me after that LSD trip, but it went beyond that. And certainly if you knew these teachings, you would not be afraid.*

Reading scriptures on one's own presents serious obstacles. The *Gītā-māhātmya* states, "One should read *Bhagavad-gītā* very scrutinizingly with the help of a person who is a devotee of Śrī Kṛṣṇa, and try to understand it without personally motivated interpretations." Similar advice is given in the *Mahābharata:* "Simply by studying the *Vedas,* which are variegated, one cannot come to the right path by which religious principles are understood"

(*Mahābharata, Vana-parva,* quoted in *Cc. Madhya* 17.186).

Problems of independent study include: (1) the scriptures of the world seem to contradict one another; (2) they are voluminous and one does not have time to go through all of them; (3) they are very grave and not open to most people's understanding.

During my ill-fated LSD trip, I had a very immediate sensation of the presence of evil. It was as if Evil personified came into the room. Afterwards, even weeks later, while lying in bed with my casts, Evil would sometimes appear again and I would become very afraid. I resorted to a homemade prayer attitude in which I turned toward a blue light that I found within myself, and prayed for protection. Perhaps I thought I was praying to the Brahman of whom I had read in the *Upāniṣads:* "He is the one light that gives light to all . . . to him who sees the Self revealed in his own heart belongs eternal bliss—to none else, to none else!" It was a kind of primitive religion of my own invention. Those who are expert and devoted to the life of prayer (such as the early Christian monks whose words are recorded in the *Philokalia*), warn that it is not possible to undertake a serious life of prayer without guidance of spiritual masters. Śrīla Prabhupāda states that just as one cannot become a recognized lawyer or doctor merely by reading books, so a devotee is recognized only when he studies with a bona fide spiritual master. I thought I knew better because of my direct perception of Evil and "the blue." But I hardly guessed how limited my realizations actually were. We may think that we have seen or experienced a great deal of spiritual life, but it is actually just a tiny glimpse, and even that has been influenced by hallucination. The reality of super-sensory phenomena is fully documented in Vedic literature. One does not have to imagine it or discover it by drugs. Inter-planetary travel, the demigods, the secrets of yoga, the all-pervading light, and the Kingdom of God—these were all beyond my dreams, and yet they are all perceivable phenomena. But one cannot enter the spiritual realm unless one hears about it from authorized literature, and accepts the disciplines of a student studying under a master.

While I was at Brooklyn college I had been disappointed when Zen author Allen Watts, spoke at our college and personally told me that enlightened states could be achieved by psychedelic drugs. Yet here I was, giving credence to insights gained on an LSD trip. I had criticized Watts to my friends saying, "How could someone attain enlightenment without undergoing discipline and study and practice?" But now "it" had happened to me, and I thought I knew better.

Nevertheless, it was auspicious that I spent the whole summer reading scriptures, as if in preparation for a religious career. I told my mother that I did not really believe in Eastern religion. Neither did I really believe in the Bible. But I was "interested." That initial interest, according to Rūpa Gosvāmī, is known as *śraddhā*, curiosity to hear the truth. It is the first step on the path of *bhakti-yoga*. The step after that is not one that you can undertake alone. You have to meet a spiritual master. As the *Vedas* state, "The solid truth of religious principles is hidden in the heart of an unadulterated self-realized person" (*Mahābharata, Vana-parva,* quoted in *Cc Madhya* 17.186). But where was I going to find a spiritual master, and how could I recognize him?

VIII

The Tibetan Book of the Dead — and Beyond

When my feet healed, I took a vacation at my parents' summer home in Avalon, New Jersey. Not having learned my lesson, I tried LSD again. This trip featured many visions of a skull and crossbones. I also explored the realm beyond death by reading The Tibetan Book of the Dead. *I do not recall where I obtained this book, but I was already browsing in that area. It had a fascinating picture in the front, of the author, W.Y. Evans-Wentz. The British university scholar was completely decked out like an Easterner and was posing with a Tibetan monk. He was smiling., One thought, "Look at that guy! He's really living with them completely!" The epigraph page stated, "Sri Krishna's Remembering," and then, "Many lives, Arjuna, both you and I have lived, I remember them all, but thou dost not." I thought, "Wow, that's a really good epigraph. This epigraph proves the whole basis of* The Tibetan Book of the Dead. *That's Kṛṣṇa from the* Bhagavad-gītā." *In the Introduction,* The Tibetan Book of the Dead *states, "This is actually a handbook that has been used by Tibetans for many centuries for what to do at the time of death. They believe that the time of death is very crucial and determines where you go next, because we have many lives." So people were supposed to intone mantras from this book and it would help them make the passage at death.*

My father had his own little dock, a narrow thing, for a rowboat. I was sitting there reading. It was sort of scary. I was reading about different Buddhas and demon-like creatures who appear at death. First you may see the Buddha of such-and-such, and he is inauspicious, so here is how you should deal with him. The next chapter would say, "In the next stage of realization, you may see the Buddha of such-and-such." I could not really understand what it was all about, what the discipline or the doctrine behind it was. But in my typically eclectic, far-out mentality, I read it with sincerity. I was not wasting time, I was interested in life after death, in Buddhas, in coming back, transcending, and in anything "far-out."

The deepest and most favorable impressions of *The Tibetan Book of the Dead* came from the book's front matter. First the photo of the "Translator and the Editor in Tibetan dress, taken in Gangtok, Sikkim." The Britisher seemed transformed into a mysterious Easterner, not only by his dress, but by the look in his eyes. There he was, with his Tibetan guru, both of them holding white roses and both absorbed in compiling the *Bardo Thödol,* "Liberation By Hearing On the After Death Plane." Never before had I guessed that a Western seeker might become so attracted to an Eastern doctrine as to become "one of them."

The first paragraph in the Preface went straight to my heart:

> That the living do come from the dead, as Socrates intuitively perceived as he was about to drink the hemlock and experience death, this treatise maintains, not in virtue of tradition or belief, but on the sound basis of the unequivocal testimony of yogins who claim to have died and re-entered the human womb consciously.

Yogīs who remember dying and being born again—it blew my mind. More than abstract arguments, this blunt assertion convinced me that it could be done. The Preface went on to say that it was very important for Western humanity to learn how to die and transcend death. It was much more important than the exploration of outer space. It was, "humanity's paramount problem, the problem of birth and death." The preface stated that the book would teach scientific and yogic understanding of desirable and undesirable after death experience. "By right practice of the art of dying, death will then, indeed, have lost its sting and been swallowed up in victory." The preface was stimulating. It readied me for an esoteric and serious treatise. But even before the book began, I found a motto which gave me more illumination than anything else in the book:

> Shri Krishna's remembering:
> "Many lives, Arjuna, you and I have lived,
> I remember them all, but thou dost not."
> —*Bhagavad-gītā*, iv, v

This was a reconfirmation of the statement that *yogīs* could experience being born again, except now it was proved by Śrī Kṛṣṇa's remembering. I did not exactly know who Śrī Kṛṣṇa was, except that He was one of the great Mystics and Authorities. He could directly experience living many lives, but others could not. The book had another preface, and this also contained a statement by Śrī Kṛṣṇa regarding "right direction of thought when dying":

> Shri Krishna, in the *Bhagavad-gītā,* viii-vi, says to Arjuna, "One attaineth whatever state [of being] one thinketh about at the last when relinquishing the body, being ever absorbed in the thought thereof."

Several times more, the "*Avatāra* Kṛṣṇa" and the *Bhagavad-gītā* were mentioned, along with the Buddha, as advocating the doctrine of pre-existence and rebirth. The edition I read contained a psychological commentary by Dr. C.G. Jung, geared to help Westerners understand Oriental teachings. Jung said that the peaceful and wrathful deities which meet the soul after death are "projections of the human psyche, an idea that seems all too obvious to the enlightened European. . . . But although the European can easily explain away these deities as projections, he would be quite incapable of positing them at the same time as real." According to Jung, *The Tibetan Book of the Dead* should be seen *both* as metaphsyical fact and as stemming from human consciousness. It was a paradox, Jung said, and if one could not handle that, he should know that he was encumbered by Occidental prejudice. I tried to accept the suggested mood of paradox as I sat in the backyard beach, facing the canal and taking breaks from my reading to join the family meals, during which time these topics were never mentioned.

When I returned to the beach for more readings, I eventually became bogged down in the confrontations with the deities that the soul meets after death, especially the wrathful ones. The first thing that one meets at death is the opportunity for the highest perfection, the supreme vision of eternal light. If one fails in that perfection, then he has to meet lesser deities, starting with the peaceful ones, and degenerating down to the wrathful ones, resulting in lower and lower rebirths. *The Tibetan Book of the Dead* was intended for reading at the time of a person's death, giving him opportunities to improve his next life, even if he should keep missing the higher chances for better re-entry. Carl Jung suggested that it would be better for a rationally-minded Western intellectual to reverse the secrets of the book, and to start at the bottom. Attempting to follow the advice, I read the book backwards to the front, struggled through a good percentage of it, not knowing whether it was real or unreal, and finally stopped.

I went away thinking it was great stuff. What I mainly retained was the conviction that death was a crucial moment and an opportunity for a next life, good or bad. Maybe I had already been sensing that in my homemade attempts at LSD meditation in a Great Kills graveyard, and the attempt to enter the blue, which had ended so painfully in the breaking of my heels. *The Tibetan Book of the Dead* was another step on this path, and although I only half-digested it, I talked about it with my friends on the Lower East Side. I decided that the subject matter was important, although difficult and elusive.

Later, when I finally met His Divine Grace Śrīla Prabhupāda, I was sufficiently influenced by *The Tibetan Book of the Dead* to think that A.C. Bhaktivedanta Swami would teach it as part of his syllabus. In my early misconceptions, I thought that Prabhupāda was offering a spiritual version of an academic course on Eastern religions, and that we would study the books of many different cultures of the East. After attending Prabhupāda's lecture for a week or two, I asked one of his followers, Raymond, whether Swamijī was going to teach *The Tibetan Book of the Dead* after we completed our study of the *Bhagavad-gītā.* Raymond smiled and said according to the Swami, the study of the *Bhagavad-gītā* was sufficient in itself. Raymond explained that the *Bhagavad-gītā* contained what was in all other scriptures, but gave new information. I was embarrassed at my foolish question, and decided to take the *Bhagavad-gītā* more seriously.

One of the great boons of studying the *Bhagavad-gītā* with Śrīla Prabhupāda was that there was no frustrating hovering between the real and the unreal. Prabhupāda made it clear that there was a spiritual reality as fully personal as the material worlds. When Śrī Kṛṣṇa discussed the individual *ātmā* as a person, and described the transmigration of the self and the Supersoul, these were not projections of human unconsciousness, but absolute truths. They were not paradoxes, but could be revealed to serious students when their minds and senses became purified. As Śrī Kṛṣṇa said, "To those who are constantly devoted to serving Me with love, I give the understanding by which they can come to Me" (*Bg.* 10.10).

Prabhupāda also defined the highest perfection in a way that satisfied me more than anything I had heard. All the Eastern teachings I had encountered, along with their commentators, spoke of impersonal merging as the highest state. Anything personal was a vestige of illusion, and had to be given up according to the texts I had read. But exactly what happened after that, in *nirvāṇa* or white-light *samādhi*, was nothing that anyone was supposed to really comprehend. It was emancipation and it was beyond all matter, *but what was it?* The words of the Buddha quoted in the *Tibetan Book of the Dead* went in the right direction, but deliberately stopped short of further information:

> There is, disciples, an Unbecome, Unborn, Unmade, Unformed; if there were not this Unbecome, Unborn, Unmade, Unformed; there would be no way out for that which is to become born, made and formed; But since there is an Unbecome, Unborn, Unmade, Unformed, there is escape for that which is become, born, made and formed.

What the *Bhagavad-gītā* taught, which was deliberately not taught by the others, and in some cases, explicitly denied by them, was that the individual *ātmā* is an eternal person. Prabhupāda drew our attention to the *Bhagavad-gītā* verse 2.12: "Never was there a time when I did not exist, nor you, nor all these kings; nor in the future shall any of us cease to be." Another important statement by Lord Kṛṣṇa was in the fifteenth chapter, verse seven: "The living entities in the conditioned world are My eternal, fragmental parts. Due to conditional life, they are struggling very hard with the six senses, which include the mind." The paradoxes and word jugglery began to clear up. Beyond the individual self, *ātmā,* is the Supreme Self, or the Paramātmā. *Both the individual self and the Supreme are persons, but the individual souls are subject to illusion and rebirth, whereas the Supreme Personality of Godhead never falls into illusion.* Authoritatively, and not too slowly, Prabhupāda brought us beyond the merely negative rejection of material desires, and taught us about the spiritual desire of the soul, transcendental loving service of the Supreme Lord.

As for a "handbook" for the time of death, it was all contained in the eighth chapter of *Bhagavad-gītā.* Whatever one thinks of at the time of death determines his next body. The personal soul takes another material body according to his karma. In the *Tibetan Book of the Dead,* the art of dying depends on how well one has lived during his lifetime. At the same time, the hour of death is a crucial one. Although the eighth chapter of *Bhagavad-gītā* contains technical information for *yogīs* as to how to leave the body at the right time through yogic manipulation, the last word of advice is that one should become a pure devotee of the Lord, and then he will not have to worry about his transference. Lord Kṛṣṇa Himself will take care of that. In his purports to these verses, Śrīla Prabhupāda repeatedly recommended the chanting of the Hare Kṛṣṇa mantra as the supreme and simple way to assure the highest emancipation after death. By chanting Kṛṣṇa's names, one will be transferred to the supreme planet, Kṛṣṇaloka, without a doubt.

> If one wants to achieve success at the end of his life, the process of remembering Kṛṣṇa is essential. Therefore, one should constantly, incessantly chant the *mahā-mantra*—Hare Kṛṣṇa Hare Kṛṣṇa Kṛṣṇa Kṛṣṇa Hare Hare/Hare Rāma Hare Rāma Rāma Rāma Hare Hare.
>
> —*Bg.* 8.5, purport

By Prabhupāda's and Lord Kṛṣṇa's grace, I am now convinced that by chanting Hare Kṛṣṇa I will not meet the wrathful deities after death, and I will be saved from the jaws of impersonal liberation.

IX

Magister Ludi, The Glass Bead Game—Spiritual Life Exists

Sometimes it seemed that I was getting warmer in my approach to the truth. But eclectic reading is such that sometimes you are up and sometimes down. Drugs also do that to you, and friendships with people who are taking drugs. I was unaware how materialistic and desperate my life had become. I was skinny, but swallowing weight-reducing pills, and my main daily meal was orange drink. The "modest" apartment I lived in was decorated by a spray-paint madman (me) who rarely had visitors. But into this "running man" existence came a ray of hope from yet another book, Magister Ludi or The Glass Bead Game, *by Herman Hesse.*

The book was dedicated to "The journeyers to the East," and as I made myself cozy on the bare floor, basking in sunlight from the fire escape, I was transported into another realm. It was the life story of Joseph Knecht, beginning with when he was a young boy and discovered that he had a calling to enter the elite school, which led to the Order. Knecht and the Order were fictional, but that was all right; it was Hesse's magic. The book even began with a fictional quote in Latin from a so-called Albert Secundus, who probably never existed, translated by Joseph Knecht:

> *Nothing is harder, yet nothing is more necessary, than to speak of certain things whose existence is neither demonstrable or probable. The very fact that serious and conscientious men treat them as existing things brings them a step closer to existence and the possiblity of being born.*

I am becoming a little fatigued of this book, *My Search Through Books,* and I suppose the Kṛṣṇa conscious reader is feeling the same. "Why hear all the doubt and unhappiness of agnostic authors and their desperate, unguided reader? Let's read Śrīla Prabhupāda." I agree. But there are only a few more of these books to go, so I suggest we stick it out together. I think there are some valuable insights we can gain from these last few books, and then we can turn to Śrīla Prabhupāda's books once and for all.

Joseph Knecht was a twelve-year-old music student. One day, he and his schoolmates learned that the country's Music Master was going to make an unprecedented visit to their little school to examine the students. Hesse endearingly described the worship of the boy for the Master, how they met and played music together. Joseph's whole being awoke on that occasion as "behind the music being created in his presence, he sensed the world of the Mind, the joy-giving harmony of law and freedom of service and rule." Joseph surrendered himself and vowed to serve that world and his Master. Hesse wrote, "He had experienced his vocation, which may surely be spoken of as a sacrament. The ideal world, which hitherto his young soul had known only by hearsay and by wild dreams had suddenly taken on visible liniments for him. Its gates had opened invitingly."

The reading had a special effect on me because of its timing in my life. I had forgotten that spiritual life existed. Directly, I no longer believed in it. All I knew was the immediate scene, the crazy pad I lived in, the hyped metabolism of my body and the sensations of Manhattan. To me, the story of Joseph Knecht and how he was accepted to an elite school to study esoteric doctrines under Masters, leading to indoctrination into a secret "Bead Game," represented spiritual life. It was nothing practical or even specific—I knew that I could not become a follower in such a school and learn the "Bead Game," and in fact, there was no such thing as a "Bead Game." But the story convinced me and mostly it *reminded* me and *woke* me up. There was somewhere a beautiful serene life, where monk-like students, those who were very exceptional and fortunate, were introduced into uplifting studies. As for the "Bead Game," it was something super-intellectual, involving mostly music and mathematics—and more. But I read *Bead Game* in my own way, fed myself on Hesse's descriptions of an existence "neither demonstrable nor probable."

The young boy was surprised to learn that he had been chosen out of millions for the privilege of entering one of the elite schools. It was a surprise to Joseph, and yet—"In spite of everything, had he not known it all along, divined it, felt it again and again? Now it had come: his raptures were confirmed, made legitimate; his sufferings had meaning . . ."

The boy left his home and local school and entered the Order, subject to its rule, which included poverty and bachelorhood. It was a monastic community excluded from competition in the world. One time, during a vacation at the school, Joseph went to visit the old Music Master, who then taught him meditation. As he pursued his studies, he was graduated to a higher school and gradually became attracted to and initiated into the secrets of the Glass Bead Game. Some derided the Bead Game as just a frivolous intellectual exercise, but Joseph saw it as a lofty, sacramental act, a sacred language for learning the secrets of existence. As Joseph wrote in a poem during his school years:

> And when we tell our beads, we serve the whole,
> And cannot be dislodged or misdirected,
> Held in the orbit of the Cosmic Soul.

The life story traced the growth and struggles of Joseph Knecht until finally he became appointed as top guru, or Magister Ludi, of the sacred secret Order. Joseph knew within himself that this would happen, even when he was first chosen as a twelve-year-old boy by his Master, and so when he was appointed to the highest post, "He felt something akin to assent, a sense that he had known and expected this all along, that it was right and natural."

The ending of the story disappointed me, and so also the three short novels which are at the end of the book, written by Joseph Knecht. The last one is set in India, with characters like Ravana, Govinda, and Dasa. On the one hand, the *Bead Game* was something wonderful, and yet it was sterile. One poem by Joseph Knecht describes "The Last Bead Game Player," an ancient master, once great, but now senile, whose beads fall futilely into the sand. So sometimes the Bead Game was derided, but sometimes he held up the vision of triumph over birth and death:

> Yet still above this vale of endless dying
> Man's spirit, struggling incorruptibly,
> Painfully raises beacons, death defying,
> And wins, by longing, immortality.

I exuberantly shared my experience of *Magister Ludi* with my friends on the Lower East Side. "It exists! Spiritual life exists!" I said. My friends were glad to see me so happy and encouraged. But when I try now to think of any practical action I took after reading *Magister Ludi,* I cannot recall it. These were ecstasies, but they led to no reform in habits, and neither did I receive any calling or meet any masters to make them something more than passing intimations of hope. Nowadays, I do not even think of them as spiritual foundations. But I cannot forget them, and so I thank them. Although it was a story book, the *Bead Game* hinted of an elite school, of a spiritual master, "his sufferings had meaning . . . ." Without such hints of something spiritual to come, I may have gone down the drain in despair.

X

I Too Could Have This If I Wanted

When I was living near the George Washington bridge, I took LSD again and had a strange experience with a book. I was reading the Duino Elegies, *by Ranier Maria Rilke, which is a book that he supposedly wrote under tremendous ecstasy of inspiration. He went and lived in a castle, which was lent to him by an aristocratic person. Rilke was waiting weeks and weeks for something to happen, and then he had an inspiration, and within a few months, he wrote this book that is considered a masterpiece. But it is very hard to understand. It is full of symbolism. I had read it a number of times. Something about it attracted me, although I could not figure it out. I was content to believe that there was something great there because "everyone" said it was, and also because I could sometimes pick it up coming through the images. There was something very sad about it, something exciting about it, and it was full of solitude.*

So I was on LSD while on the subway. I was standing on the subway platform waiting for the train and I thought, "I will read Rilke now. It will be good to read while you are in this intense state." I opened the book up and started to read a page which I had read a number of times before. Then something exploded in me or in the book. Rilke himself had said, "Don't think I write things because I just think them up, but rather, I experience them." This was a shock, an explosion of potency—I was able to commune with what was being said. Of course, it was the LSD working, producing a super-conscious state so that what you feel becomes actually true—*which is, I think, the meaning of hallucination.*

I was communing with what Rilke was saying. He had written for an audience, and he was writing from such a deep place—and I was getting it. *The sensation of exploding was just as real as the loud noise of the subway train approaching and the train's headlight. As real as that, was this explosion that occurred, and it was so violent that I had to close the book. I could not read when something was exploding! I was appreciative of it, and in awe of it, but it was frightening. You are going to explode to bits if you go on like this! And the message was*—that he was so lonely and it was such a fearful place. *It was too much. And I too could have this if I wanted it.*

I was hallucinating. Rilke was inspired by his Muse, flying in his imagination. So a great poet and a tiny poet met and exploded in mid-air. My LSD reading of Rilke is an extreme case of what can be achieved in communing with an author who has passed away, but has conveyed his spirit in writing. Yet the *Duino Elegies* could not deliver me to peace and truth. At best, I was able to share deep, powerful intimations, like blows to the spirit. The poet's power overcame me and I sensed that if I read further, I would "explode." Rilke was millions of times more a poet than I would ever be. But as I looked into his soul while standing on the subway platform, I saw that he was a mortal, troubled man. He could not bless me with love of God. I would have to search further before I would find an author who could save me.

Epilogue

As I came down from my Rilke-explosion trip, my body gave me messages of ill health; something wasn't right. The life of the hunger artist and LSD-tripping was taking its toll. My parents saw my life in the city as child's play, but I knew that the stakes I was playing with were high. At this rate, how long could I last?

This happened in 1965. At the same time, His Divine Grace Śrīla Prabhupāda was about to start his journey on the Jaladuta to America:

Now only the ocean's storms
separated you from us.
On our side,
the hour was very late,
but not too late.
No one was waiting for you in exactly the form
you were coming,
yet we were aching for you nonetheless—
as parched land awaits rain,
as a lost child awaits the mother,
as a lonely lover awaits the beloved,
as the soul aches for God.
The dumb tongues stuck,
unable to utter "Kṛṣṇa,"
the blind groped,
the mad went madder, incurring reactions;
and every moment more *jīvas* fell
off the cliff of human life, down
into the abyss of *tamo-guṇa.*

Afterword

The message of this book is not, "Ain't I smart to have read so many books?" It is, "I survived. I made it to his lotus feet." Otherwise, I am not clever for having read a number of non-Vaiṣṇava books.

You don't have to go through what I did. There is no particular advantage. When I am giving a *Śrīmad-Bhāgavatam* lecture, I can make an occasional reference to Franz Kafka, but that's no big deal, is it? Better to have been educated in Sanskrit.

I am relieved to have told this tale. I hope it will be useful to others.

This book has been completed in Ireland where I have been traveling and preaching. Now I plan to spend a few days exclusively reading Śrīla Prabhupāda's books. I read them every day. They are my life and soul. He is the author I was searching for.

St. Finan's Bay, Kerry
Ekādaśī, March 11, 1991

GLOSSARY

A

ācārya—a spiritual master who teaches by example.

B

bhakti-yoga—linking with the Supreme Lord through devotional service.

brahmacārī—a celibate student.

brāhmaṇa—one wise in the *Vedas* who can guide others; the first Vedic social order.

D

dhāma—abode, place of residence, usually referring to the Lord's abode.

G

gṛhastha—regulated householder life; the second order of Vedic spiritual life.

J

japa—soft, private chanting of the holy names.

K

Kali-yuga—The Age of Kali; the present age, characterized by quarrel; it is the last in the cycle of four ages and began five thousand years ago.

karma—fruitive action, for which there is always reaction, good or bad.

kīrtana—chanting the glories of the Supreme Lord.

M

mantra—a sound vibration that can deliver the mind from illusion.

māyā—(*mā*-not; *yā*-this), illusion; forgetfulness of one's relationship with Kṛṣṇa.

S

sādhana—regulated spiritual practices.

sannyāsī—a person in the renounced order of life; the fourth spiritual order in Vedic society.

śāstra—revealed scripture.

V

Vṛndāvana—the transcendental abode of Lord Kṛṣṇa.

Acknowledgements

I would like to thank the following friends and disciples who have helped to produce and print this book:

Rukmavatī-devī dāsī, Bhakta Rob Head, Kaiśorī-devī dāsī, and Madana-mohana dāsa.

Special thanks to Navadvīpa dāsa for his kind donation to print this book.

Other Books by Satsvarūpa dāsa Goswami

Readings in Vedic Literature
A Handbook for Kṛṣṇa Consciousness
He Lives Forever
Śrīla Prabhupāda-līlāmṛta (Vols. 1-6)
Distribute Books, Distribute Books, Distribute Books
The Twenty-six Qualities of a Devotee/
Vaiṣṇava Behavior
With Śrīla Prabhupāda in the Early Days: A Memoir (formerly titled: Letters From Śrīla Prabhupāda)
Japa Reform Notebook
The Voices of Surrender and Other Poems
Remembering Śrīla Prabhupāda (Vols. 1-5)
Life With the Perfect Master
In Praise of the Mahājanas and Other Poems
Prabhupāda Nectar (Vols. 1-5)
Living With the Scriptures
Reading Reform Notebook
The Worshipable Deity and Other Poems
Under the Banyan Tree
Dust of Vṛndāvana
Journal and Poems (Books 1-3)
Guru Reform Notebook

(other books cont.)

Prabhupāda-līlā

Pictures From the Bhagavad-gītā As It Is and Other Poems

Lessons From the Road (Vols. 1-17)

Iṣṭa-goṣṭhī (Vols. 1-3)

Nimāi dāsa and the Mouse: A Fable

Nimāi's Detour

Gurudeva and Nimāi: Struggling for Survival

Choṭa's Way

Truthfulness, The Last Leg of Religion

Prabhupāda Meditations (Vols. 1-2)

Prabhupāda Appreciation

ISKCON in the 1970s: Diaries (vol. 1 & 2)

Memory in the Service of Kṛṣṇa

Obstacles on the Path of Devotional Service

Talking Freely With My Lords